Shackled by a Heavy Burden

Shackled by a Heavy Burden

An Examination of Barriers Pastors Face when Providing Pastoral Counseling or Referrals in the African American Church

KENNARD MURRAY

RESOURCE *Publications* · Eugene, Oregon

SHACKLED BY A HEAVY BURDEN
An Examination of Barriers Pastors Face when Providing Pastoral Counseling or Referrals in the African American Church

Copyright © 2011 Kennard Murray. All rights reserved. Except for brief quotations in critical publications or reviews, no part of this book may be reproduced in any manner without prior written permission from the publisher. Write: Permissions, Wipf and Stock Publishers, 199 W. 8th Ave., Suite 3, Eugene, OR 97401.

Resource Publications
An Imprint of Wipf and Stock Publishers
199 W. 8th Ave., Suite 3
Eugene, OR 97401
www.wipfandstock.com

ISBN 13: 978-1-60899-924-8

Manufactured in the U.S.A.

All scripture quotations, unless otherwise indicated, are taken from the Holy Bible, New International Version®, NIV®. Copyright ©1973, 1978, 1984 by Biblica, Inc.™ Used by permission of Zondervan. All rights reserved worldwide.

Contents

Preface vii
Acknowledgments xiii
Glossary xv

1. Statement of the Problem / Research Question 1
2. Significance of the Problem of Resistance 9
3. Theological Perspective 33
4. Methodology 43
5. Findings 50
6. Conclusion 78

   Appendix A 87
   Appendix B 91
   Appendix C 93
   Appendix D 95
   Appendix E 137
   Bibliography 141

Preface

IN 1993 when I first was appointed to pastor a local church I saw myself as a pastor who provided counseling to my parishioners on short term crisis, pre-marital, grief, and marital counseling. My training in Divinity School had prepared me for these situations appropriately and I felt I was effective. But then came a deeper calling which other pastors may experience but do not know what it is or how to answer.

I realized I was being called to the "specialized ministry of pastoral counseling" within the first five years of being appointed to pastor churches in the United Methodist Church. I was a local pastor serving a charge (appointed pastor of two or more churches) in my home state of Tennessee. In the course of the three years I served as pastor of one particular charge, I was confronted with two cases wherein persons were just beginning to get in touch with the emotional pain of being sexually abused as young children. They came to me, their pastor, for help and I was not prepared to provide the appropriate care and counsel because their issues were beyond my scope of training. Although I had several courses in pastoral care and counseling during my theological training, the trauma these adult women were finally attempting to process was beyond my training at that time. In the practice of ministry, I knew it best to refer persons with special needs to qualified counseling professionals in the community. In these two cases I made numerous appropriate referrals but the persons refused to go to the appointment with professional counselors, though they had agreed. It became apparent to me they had resistance in sharing their stories with professional pastoral counselors or professional counselors. Without failure they returned to me, their pastor, for relief from the emotional distress they were experiencing. I felt as if I was shackled by a heavy burden. I learned in the African American church there are several barriers to making successful referrals to agencies in the larger community. One barrier is that many African Americans are resistant to secular counseling; and secondly, in some cases the lack of skill and sensitivity to provide contextual counseling by the pastoral counselor or other counseling professionals is a major problem.

Often the failure to receive professional help is due to a combination of the two. After further reflection I discerned this was part of my calling and I needed specialized training in the field of pastoral counseling and psychotherapy. Further, I wondered if other pastors experienced the same problem of resistance in referring their parishioners. During my training in the field of pastoral counseling and psychotherapy I was drawn to learning more about the dynamic of resistance. Why would some persons in the African American community refuse to take their stories and pain outside the pastor's study to a professional counselor? My interest in the African American community was primarily because this is where I first experienced the dynamics of resistance. I am United Methodist. Although the denomination's membership is predominantly white according to the 2006 U.S. ethnic lay membership data there are 444,141

African American members and counting, the majority of whom worship in predominately African American congregations. Further my observations of the silent suffering of persons in mental and emotional pain come from serving predominately African American congregations. However, when I proposed this research project I was suprised that I had to address the appropriateness of my speaking on the Black Church experience since I was a member of a larger predominately white denomination. I remember the late Rev. Dr. Samuel Dewitt Proctor addressed a national audience of preachers, scholars, and church leaders assembled from throughout the Black Church in 1992 at the opening ceremony of a conference titled, "What Does It Mean To Be Black And Christian," sponsored by the Kelly Miller Smith Institute on the Black Church and Vanderbilt University Divinity School. Dr. Proctor shared the Black Church is of a great variety and includes black congregations within a larger fellowship which is predominantly white. That is one kind of experience. He went on to explain how all predominantly Black Church denominations came into existence. Dr. Proctor made a point of showing that we all have a distinctive origin, but we are the Black Church with one common thread running through it "this institution is the spiritual mother and the nurturing agent of this black people with this peculiar history." I believe the findings of the study I conducted in 2008 are relevant to the African American church today, regardless of denominational affiliation.

My interest began to focus on other African American pastors' experiences of providing pastoral counseling in the parish or referring parishioners to professional counselors in the community. I was particularly interested to learn if they also experienced resistance in making referrals to professional counselors. Further, I was curious to learn if they felt as ill equipped to help as I did at the beginning of this journey. My intention in conducting this study and now sharing my findings in this book is not to communicate directly or indirectly that resistance to referral to professional counselors is only an African American problem. In the African American experience there are numerous factors such as racism, mistrust of agencies outside the African American community, stigma of needing professional mental health services, cultural taboos in the media concerning mental illness, fear of being placed on psychotropic medication, lack of empathy and lack of financial resources which play a major role in many African Americans' resistance to professional counseling. I believe there are people in the majority church as well as other ethnic congregations who struggle with the same issues of resistance to professional counseling; although the source of their resistance may not be for many of the same reasons as African Americans. Even as resistance is evident in many congregations from the pulpit to the pews regardless of ethnicity, my context is the African American church.

Nevertheless the field of psychology has not always been welcomed with open arms in the majority faith community either. In the summer of 2007 I attended the annual Festival of Homiletics. That year it was held in Nashville, Tennessee. One of the great preachers of our generation and retired professor, Rev. Dr. Fred Craddock preached a sermon on Hyperbole. He recalled years ago at the end of the last century reading a sermon by a preacher from Kentucky describing this new discipline that had just been introduced into the schools called psychology. Rev. Craddock recalled this preacher describing this new discipline to a congregation in his sermon as being compared to "a blind man in a dark cellar at midnight with a flashlight looking for a black cat that was not there!" In order to give a larger view of resistance I will touch on resistance in the majority faith community regarding psychology, pastoral counseling and clinical pastoral therapy; but the thrust of this humble attempt is to add to the conversation of Pastoral Counseling in the African American Church with a focus on the experiences of African Americans.

Acknowledgments

I WANT to first thank my family for their support, patience, and encouragement in many ways during this doctoral program and research project, my wife Pamela and children Keith, Marc, Tiffany, and Kenny.

Secondly, I want to thank my church family, the members of the Seay-Hubbard United Methodist Church (Nashville, TN) and all the congregations I have been appointed to serve as pastor since 1993 in the Tennessee Annual Conference of the United Methodist Church. Thank you for allowing me to be your shepherd and spiritual leader. Also this journey could not have been made without the support of the Pastoral Counseling Centers of Tennessee where I received my clinical training and supervision and the General Board of Higher Education & Ministry, Division of Ordained Ministry Section of Chaplains And Related Ministries. Thank you for your faith in me and believing in the importance of this work.

Finally, to all my friends and colleagues, thank you for your encouragement and support especially to Rev. Elbrist Mason, Mr. Arthur Hyde, and to the six clergy participants who freely gave of their time and shared their experiences counseling those persons who sit in our pews shackled by heavy burdens.

Glossary

Boundaries—Creating clear lines of professional distance with counselee, where the counselor does not crossover into personal or inappropriate sexual or emotional areas in the counselee's life or the counselee is not allowed to crossover into personal or inappropriate sexual or emotional areas in the counselor's life. Boundaries are rules that help maintain the safety and integrity of the pastoral counseling relationship. Boundary violations can be sexual, emotional or both.

Clinical Pastoral Education (CPE) —is professional education for ministry which brings theological students, ordained clergy, members of religious orders, and qualified laypersons into supervised encounters with what Anton Boisen called the living human documents, or persons, in order to develop their pastoral identity, inter-personal competence, and spirituality; the skills of pastoral assessment, interprofessional collaboration, group leadership, pastoral care, and counseling; and pastoral theological reflection. "Dictionary of Pastoral Care & Counseling pp. 177–78"

Counseling Pastor—a pastor while in the course of everyday duties provides limited crisis counseling to members of the parish regarding issues such as marital problems, adjusting to changes of life, grief, illnesses, premarital counseling, etc. At the appropriate time if the problems that the members are dealing with are beyond the pastor's scope of training he/she will refer to a professional counselor.

Countertransference—The pastoral counselor or the counseling pastor's feelings and reactions, both positive and negative, towards the person seeking counseling. These feelings can be sexual attraction, anger, or emotional overinvolvement. These feelings can interfere with the counseling process if not addressed by supervision.

Dual Relationship—When the pastor develops both a pastoral relationship and a long term counseling relationship with a member of the congregation, thereby creating two distinct and conflicting relationships with the parishioner: both their pastor and counselor. Dual relationships can lead to ethical and other boundary violations.

Gatekeeper—a professional who can control the entry of a person in need of specialized services to the service delivery system; professionals such as social workers, teachers, guidance counselors, pastors, etc.

Pastoral Counselor—a pastor engaged in the specialized ministry of pastoral counseling, pastoral psychotherapy, and other work of personal healing or growth, often in collaboration with other mental health professionals, utilizing the insights and principles from the disciplines of theology and the behavioral sciences. "Dictionary of Pastoral Care & Counseling p.855"

Professional counselor or pastoral counselor—someone trained in the disciplines of psychotherapy and theology. Further, these persons have met the necessary standards and been granted credentials by the appropriate governing body. The credentials would be certification or licensure.

Resistance—a person's unwillingness to get in touch with their unconscious feelings or memories that cause them pain. This unwillingness could manifest in therapy or by refusing to go to therapy.

Transference—In the context of pastoral counseling, the phenomenon of the transference of distorted feelings or emotions from unresolved childhood family of origin relationships of the person seeking counseling to the pastoral counselor or the counseling pastor. These feelings can be positive or negative.

Note: The majority of these definitions were learned during the course of my clinical training and supervision.

1

Statement of the Problem / Research Question

WHAT ARE some of the reasons many African Americans will share their pathologies and other psychological problems with their pastor, but will not follow through if the pastor makes an appropriate referral to receive clinical help from a professional pastoral counselor or other qualified counseling professional?

The Black Church has historically been the institution that African Americans have always turned to in times of need. A people's emotional and mental health needs are no exception. The Black Church is that institution which has always been the stabilizing presence in the African American community. The Black Church's genesis was in the slave quarters where slaves gathered to console and be supportive in their common plight. The Black Church was the principle agent of change during the periods of reconstruction, the civil unrest of the 1960s, and post September 11, 2001. The Black Church is the source of strength and perseverance, and most importantly a place in which one obtains hope that life will get better.

The African American pastor has been designated preacher, teacher, leader, political spokesperson, fundraiser, organizer, and pastoral care provider throughout the centuries. This role has historically placed the pastor in a real position of power and overwhelming responsibility that most African American pastors have handled well, although some have not. The pastor is still seen as the first person outside the home to whom a person can take their problems in order to receive help and advice.

There is still mistrust in the African American community regarding many social service agencies. The pastor's advice, in many cases, is sought out before help or contact with a social service agency is made. These precautions are taken because many social services systems are complex and perceived as lacking empthy. Many times when social services agencies get involved with family issues their involvement becomes invasive. Many families have experienced control over family members or situations being taken away from them by social agencies. Frequently, parental and other rights are suspended by government authority. When this happens the family system becomes over burdened with helplessness and many times they must find representation by attorneys to fight to get their rights back. Seeking legal help compounds their problems became now the family is faced with another financial drain that in many cases they can not afford. Therefore, seeking help from a respected and sensitive pastor is far more likely to be their best avenue in times of crisis than going to a social services agency.

The following facts clarify how often the local pastor, regardless of race, is confronted with people seeking counseling. An article in the *Journal of Marital and Family Therapy*, written by Weaver, Koenig, and Larson, concludes: "Pastors are the primary mental health counselors for tens of millions of Americans."¹ This report clearly shows that clergy are the most trusted professionals in society. In the book, *Counseling Families Across the Stages of Life: A Handbook for Pastors and Other Helping Professionals,* Weaver, Revilla, and Koenig identify the clergy not only as the primary mental health counselors for the masses, but claim that they are the initial contact in times of marital troubles:

> The 22,000 members of the American Association of Marriage and Family Therapists are outnumbered by clergy sixteen to one (Weaver, Koenig, and Larson, 1997). Not surprisingly, clergypersons serve as marriage and family counselors for millions of Americans, based on accessibility alone. In thirteen separate studies conducted between 1979 and 1992, it was found that those who seek pastoral counsel bring concerns predominantly related to marriage and family issues (Weaver et al., 1997). Wasman, Corradi, and Clemens (1979) report that 85 percent of parish-based clergy indicated that family problems were the most frequent and most difficult counseling issues they were asked to address. ²

These studies are reflecting the role the pastor has in the eyes of the community across cultural boundaries. Finally,

1. A. J. Weaver, H. G. Koenig, and D.B. Larson, "Marital and Family Therapist and the Clergy: A Need for Clinical Collaboration, Training and Research," *Journal of Marital and Family Therapy,* 1997, Vol.23, No.1, pp.13–25.

2. A. J. Weaver, L. A. Revilla, and H.G. Koenig, *Counseling Families Across the Stages of Life: A Handbook for Pastors and Other Helping Professionals* (Nashville,TN: Abingdon Press, 2002) p.19.

the National Institute of Mental Health (Hohmann and Larson 1993 p.71.) concludes that:

> Clergy are as likely as mental health specialists to have a person with a Diagnostic and *Statistical Manual of Mental Disorders* diagnosis come to them for help. Clergy are seen for assistance with even the most severe forms of mental illness, including schizophrenia and bi-polar disorder.[3]

These citations alone show how frequently the public, as well as the congregants, utilize pastors in the role of counselor, given the clergy's accessibility, interpersonal skills and the level of trust that our society places in the clergy.

I have observed after being a pastor for seventeen years that many parishioners will not seek professional counseling. They sit in their pews Sunday after Sunday silently suffering. These people fall through the cracks. I have observed several reasons for this. The reasons are lack of such services in their community, inability to pay for such services, or the lack of trust to seek help from outside the family or pastor. These concerns, real or unfounded, exist. Many people do not seek help outside their community. It has been my experience that many pastoral counseling centers are located in churches in affluent communities and are not easily accessible to the poor. Added to this fact is the lack of African American pastoral counselors on staff to provide services from a contextual perspective.

---

3. A. A. Hohmann and D. B. Larson, "Psychiatric Factors Predicting Use of Clergy," in E. L. Worthington, Jr. (Ed.), *Psychotherapy and Religious Values* (Grand Rapid, MI: Baker Book House, 1993), pp. 71–84.

Statement of the Problem / Research Question 5

As Americans deal with the pressures of post 9/11/01, these pressures create worries about the safety of families and one's future. The threat of another attack on United States soil is a real possibility. The belief that Americans are safe from terrorism is gone forever. Future terrorist attacks will most likely be in large populated cites where large numbers of African Americans reside. The long-term post trauma of the 9/11/01 attack is still being assessed. The military response to this event resulted in young men and women going to war in two countries, Afghanistan and Iraq, with no end in sight in Afghanistan and thankfully the combat mission ended on August 18, 2010 in Iraq with 50,000 troops remaining as advisors with no end in sight. Military families are feeling the effects of war and loved ones returning home mentally and/or physically wounded, or dead. The military has been an avenue of upward mobility for many African Americans. Also young men and women joined the Reserves branch of the military to make additional income. Like most people who joined the Reserves, African Americans joined rarely thinking they would be mobilized for active duty for extended periods of time jeopardizing their full time employment. The emotional and economic burdens on the family system are more strained than pre 9/11/2001. As listed above these pressures are compounded in the African American community. The old saying is still true today, "if America catches a cold the African American community catches pneumonia."

The effects of living in United States society today are visible in the pathologies present in African Americans who seek pastoral counseling just as they are in persons in the majority (white) community. Nevertheless, because of the important role the pastor has in the African American community, persons seeking help from distress, crisis, and depression, first, and many times only, turn to their pastor.

Early in my ministry it became apparent I could not do all that was expected of me as pastor and provide more than brief supportive pastoral counseling. Frequently, some parishioners needed quality narrative therapy, as well as clinical psychodynamic therapy integrated into a theological framework. Unfortunately, there were no African American Clinical Pastoral Therapists in Middle Tennessee to whom I could make appropriate referrals for treatment. I made referrals to other agencies, but many parishioners would not follow through because of feelings of a lack of trust, empathy, and economic constraints.

There was a tension between the church's inability to care for persons struggling with lack of clinical pastoral help and with my identity as pastor. I had been told in my clinical residency program that pastors should not have a dual relationship with congregants and to always refer to appropriate resources outside of church. That solution is incongruent with my understanding of the African American church being the healing agent as well as the agent of change in the community. Now that I see myself as a Pastoral Theologian, I feel more congruent in my call to provide counseling to those who fall through the cracks. Traditionally the African American church has been the institution where African Americans could turn for help regardless of the situation. Throughout the Black Church's history it has been the sustaining institution to which people could turn for help in every aspect of life, such as spiritual, emotional, educational, financial, and political guidance and instruction. It was not common for persons within the church to take referrals from their pastors to seek additional help at the pastoral counseling centers. There is a need for *a congregational-based counseling paradigm* that fills the void between the church and the pastoral counseling center.

Chapter 2 defines the term resistance in the context of the research project I conducted in 2007. This chapter will review the literature on people's resistance to being referred to professional counselors and the reasons why. The importance of this topic will be explain and discussed. This chapter will investigate a representative sample of clergy attitudes regarding their counseling responsibilities and whether they are adequately trained to help people with mental and emotional issues. Clergy's referral process will be examined and their awareness of existing community mental health services will be reviewed.

Chapter 3 gives the theological perspective. In the African American church tradition, the pastor in teaching and counseling members has always used the Holy Bible. The Holy Bible is abundant with narratives of every human condition possible. People desire to have their feelings and problems interpreted through the lens of the scriptures. Also, this chapter will highlight a model of pastoral counseling that uses the Bible as a counseling tool.

Chapter 4 is the methodology chapter. In this study I selected the qualitative research method. I wanted to obtain data from clergy's stories about their counseling experiences and making referrals to professional counselors.

Chapter 5 is a summary of findings with clergy participants about their counseling experiences. The benefits from understanding the resistance to professional counseling will be outlined in this chapter. I will share the themes or patterns that were observed during the interview process with the six clergy participants. There are several tables listing all themes, recurring themes, major themes, and minor themes. Following the tables will be several quotes from the interviews citing these themes in the participants' own words. Finally, Attachment D contains two complete interviews of participants.

Chapter 6 is the conclusion. I will recommend several approaches to the problems of resistance to seeking professional counseling. This chapter also lists areas where further research would be beneficial to the church universal.

2

Significance of the Problem of Resistance

THE TEXTBOOK definition of resistance states that this phenomenon is a person's unwillingness to get in touch with their unconscious feelings or memories that cause them pain. However, this type of resistance was not the focus of my research project. There is a phenomenon of resistance where a person refuses to seek counseling or help beyond what the pastor will or is able to give. My research examines the form of resistance seen when people present themselves to their pastor for help or healing caused by some mental or emotional discomfort. When the pastor attempts to refer the person to a qualified trained professional they refuse to seek that help. In this chapter I will explore the reasons for their unwillingness to obtain needed help from a trained professional. The primary aim of this investigation was to ascertain what issues affect the parishioner's decision not to seek help from someone other than the pastor.

My hypothesis was that some African American parishioners resist counseling from professional counselors for two reasons: 1) a history of racism and cultural insensitivity in the mental health system; 2) a lack of education and training by African American pastors and church leaders. This resistance is manifested in the African American community by fear, shame, lack of empathy and trust, being judged and fear of being labeled "crazy" or mentally ill because of a misperception of the purposes of professional counseling. These reasons mainly exist because of mandatory counseling forced by social welfare agencies and courts and in general because of a misperception of the purposes of professional counseling. I will explain these two reasons further by looking at racism and the incompetence of the mental health system in understanding and serving African Americans, and as related to training of clergy and church leaders regarding professional counseling. It was anticipated that the majority of pastors would feel unequipped to provide the level of counseling those seeking counseling needed and that they would not know what referral resources were available in the community; although a small percentage would feel they do provide counseling on a professional level.

WHY DO PEOPLE TURN TO THEIR PASTOR FOR MENTAL HEALTH COUNSELING?

At the onset clarification needs to be made about why people first turn to the pastor. Paul Pruyser states in his book "*The Minister As Diagnostician*," that some people turn to their priest or minister to seek help from the safety of the faith group first and go outside their faith group only in order to receive the help they need. People tend to turn to persons they trust such as family members and community leaders before they go to faceless bureaucrats. Pruyser states:

> Their beliefs drive them into the study of their pastor. They want their problems sized up and

> tackled within a definite frame of reference. They want their tradition to speak to them, they want to discuss themselves in familiar terms; they want a glimpse of the light of their faith to clarify their predicament.[1]

This was the problem I faced while serving a Charge (pastor of two or more churches) in the Tennessee Annual Conference of the United Methodist Church. I was approached twice within two years by women congregants who were ready and felt safe enough to work on their childhood trauma of being victims of incest. I referred to my seminary training in pastoral counseling. I went to the *Dictionary of Pastoral Care and Counseling* (Rodney J. Hunter 1990 p.574–575) seeking direction in the definition of "incest" and there found the appropriate instructions:

> Adults victimized as children may have unresolved feelings of anger and betrayal along with a variety of residual after effects. Many individuals carry their secret for years; until recently, their needs often have been ignored or dismissed by professionals who regarded reports of incest as oedipal fantasies without basis in fact…The pastoral counselor is advised to refer to mental health or social service professionals specializing in incest problems.[2]

Equipped with these instructions, I tried to refer these victims of incest to professionals in the community only

---

1. P. W. Pruyser, *The Minister as Diagnostician* (Philadelphia, PA Westminster Press, 1976), p. 47.

2. Rodney J. Hunter, Dictionary Of Pastoral Care And Counseling, (Nashville, Abingdon Press, 1990), pp. 574–75.

to realize, after several attempts, that they refused to take their sacred stories, with their pain and shame, outside the pastor's office. This chapter will examine some of the issues in the majority community, and particularly in the African American community, that pastors must overcome to make appropriate mental health referrals to parishioners. This chapter will also discuss what research has been conducted regarding these issues in the African American community.

RACISM WITHIN MENTAL HEALTH THEORIES, PRACTICES, AND SYSTEMS

Racism affects every aspect of the African American experience in the United States. Therefore, it should not be surprising that racism can be found in the field of mental health through its theories, practices and systems. Nancy Boyd-Franklin addresses this fact in her book, *Black Families in Therapy: Understanding The African American Experience*. Racism is the cause of many of the issues facing African Americans seeking help beyond the family and pastor. Many African Americans are fearful that seeking therapy will result in their being labeled "crazy." This is not a myth, but fact. In my personal experience of going through a divorce and fighting to maintain primary custody of my two minor sons, I sought help from a Christian Counseling Center. This became an issue that was used in the legal process in an unsuccessful attempt to prove I was unfit as a single parent. But because I worked in the mental health field I did not let the fear of this labeling deter me from fighting for custody of my sons. This unfortunately has not been the case for many people who fear that the legal system, family, friends, and the community will conclude that they are emotionally unstable because they sought professional help in coping with stages of life. African American families are often not self-referred, meaning some social welfare agency or other public entity such as schools, courts, or hospitals have sent them for treatment under pressure. African Americans, like many other ethnic groups, are private people, teaching their children not to share what happens in the family to outsiders. This is evident in one of the two cases I shared of parishioners coming to me as their pastor for help as adults dealing with incidents of childhood incest. One woman, as a teenager, was hospitalized on a psychiatric unit by both parents when she shared what her father was doing to her sexually. They stated she was making up these stories on her father and needed psychological help for lying. The young woman was forced to recant what she had reported to the authorities as a condition for her parents to have her discharged from the psychiatric facility. This example illustrates how seriously children may be taught the lesson of keeping family business in the home. Historically the reputation of mental health services has been used as a form of social control for poor people and minorities.

These two groups' fears of being labeled as psychotic and given psychotropic drugs, as well as the inability to pay for services, prohibits them from seeking outside help. The African American community has a negative history of dealing with the welfare system and of other social agencies going beyond their legal boundaries into the private business of the family. Another reason for resistance by African American families is the perception that the family must keep "family secrets" private. Boyd-Franklin's section on Family Secrets states:

> The type of secret that is kept from certain members within the family is the more toxic and difficult to explore. They are often unconscious, obscure, or nebulous. Often these secrets have been passed down over generations (Bowen, 1976; Nichols & Schwartz, 1998). It is not unusual to discover that family members are aware of the secrets or loaded issues that are never discussed. These secrets take many forms and often do not surface until one is very far along in the treatment process. The issue of secrecy has serious clinical implications. The following secrets are some of the most common that therapists will encounter: (1) informal adoption and secrets about true parentage; (2) fatherhood; (3) unwed pregnancy; (4) a parent who had "trouble" at an earlier age; (5) an ancestor who was mentally ill, alcoholic, or a drug abuser; (6) ancestors (particularly White ones); and (7) skin color issues. These may be secrets kept from other family members, particularly the younger generation, or they may be toxic or loaded areas in the present family system that are never discussed.[3]

The power of secrets and the fear of judgment by outsiders surface in counseling with all groups. This form of resistance is seen particularly in women of every racial, ethnic, religious, geographical, and economical background. In *The Handbook of Womencare: Through the Eyes of Women*, edited by Jeanne Stevenson Moessner, Emma J. Justes (1996) of

3. Ibid., pp. 25–26.

Northern Baptist Theological Seminary examined how the social system has shaped how older women of every racial background hold on to the secrets of being abused sexually and physically all their adult lives and in the later stages of life begin to talk about these experiences with their pastors. Justes' section on The Reality of Women's Secrets states:

> The woman described above shared a painful memory of an experience of incest that occurred seventy years earlier. Other women carry secrets that are equally painful and equally enduring. Some women, now widowed, spent their entire lifetimes of marriage experiencing emotional and/or physical abuse from their husbands. They may never have told anyone. Still other women have lived married lives raising children with a nagging awareness that their true sexual identity was lesbian (even if they had no such label for it). Still others may carry secret experiences of rape or other forms of sexual abuse outside the family. Some women have taken on roles of caregivers in their families of origin, forgoing a family of their own to tend the needs of ill or aging parents, while other siblings married, moved away, and raised children of their own. While women graciously take on this role, some of them may hold secret regrets or resentments.[4]

According to this article these older women are beginning to share the sacred stories with pastors who have served in the church for long periods of time. The events that trigger

---

4. Jeanne Stevenson Moessner, edited, *The Handbook of Womencare: Through the Eyes of Women Insights For Pastoral Care*, (Minneapolis: Fortress Press 1996), pp. 241–42.

older women to talk for the first time about their secrets often are a series of adult classes dealing with human sexuality and the trust level they have with their pastor.

In my research I found resistance, as previously defined, to be quoted more frequently in the literature dealing directly with the African American community. Nancy Boyd-Franklin warns that there must be a professional respect between therapy and religion, if not, conflicts will surface:

> Many African Americans will seek pastoral counseling through their churches (Wimberly, 1997). Therapy, however, is often seen as very secular. Therapists should also be aware that some very religious African American clients may view therapy as " antispiritual" and that this may cause conflicts for some of these clients about being in therapy (Boyd-Franklin & Lockwood, 1999). Throughout its history, the mental health field has often pathologized religious or spiritual individuals (Bergin & Jensen, 1990). Because of this history and the secularity of treatment modalities, very religious clients (and their ministers) may be suspicious of therapy and may be concerned that the therapist will not respect their religious beliefs (Boyd-Franklin & Lockwood, 1999). In these situations, it is very important that the therapist encourage the client and his or her family to discuss their concerns. In some cases, this can result in the family feeling more trust toward the therapist and choosing to continue in treatment. Sometimes, getting the family's permission to consult their minister can help with this process of joining. In other situations,

> some very religious African American families have requested a referral to a Christian therapist. If this occurs, the clinician should respect their request and help to expedite the referral.[5]

This discussion has so far dealt with African American women and the phenomenon of resistance. The focus will now turn to African American men's resistance to mental health services. In Daniel Troy Hembree's doctoral dissertation (2003), *Person, Community and Divinity in Yoruba Religious Thought and Culture: Foundations for Pastoral Theology With African American Men,* he quotes from the American Counseling Association's report entitled "Counseling African American Men" regarding resistance in African American men:

> Help-seeking attitudes and behaviors among African American men. In considering issues of counseling with African American men, it is important to examine their help-seeking attitudes and behaviors. Consistent with the literature on counseling men in general, African American men, as a rule, do not seek counseling. In many cases, African American men consider the need to seek traditional counseling as an admission of weakness or as "unmanly." Although this is a phenomenon that can be observed among men from a number of racial or ethnic groups, it takes on a different dimension for African American men. For many of them, doing anything that seems unmanly can threaten a positive self-concept already diminished by society's views and stereotypes of African American personhood.

---

5. Ibid., pp. 140–41.

> As a rule, therefore, African American men are generally socialized not to open up to strangers.
>
> Other issues. In many instances, African American men are referred for counseling by some societal agent—judge, social worker, or probation officer—after they have committed some offense against the social order. Counseling, therefore, become for these men a forced process, and the implicit goal is rehabilitation or punishment. Many other African American men also approach the counseling process with apathy, suspicion, or hostility. The resistant attitude about counseling may be a defense mechanism among African American males because they generally view counseling as an activity conducted by agents of a system that has rendered them virtually powerless, the counseling process can seem to be just one more infringement on African American manhood.[6]

This report clearly states that men in general resist counseling, but for African American men there are added burdens. The stereotype of African American males and the self-image would be viewed as negative. The African American male struggles to do all within his power not to be viewed as unmanly, therefore, being referred to a professional counselor would be resisted. I, as a pastoral counselor, have clients who were referred through the legal system or human service agencies. It has been my experience that it is very difficult to develop the therapeutic relationship with

6. Daniel Troy Hembree, *Person, Community and Divinity in Yoruba Religious Thought and Culture: Foundations for Pastoral Theology With African American Men*, Dissertation (Northwestern University 2003), p. 172.

Significance of the Problem of Resistance 19

these clients in order to achieve serious supportive or insight oriented therapy. They viewed me as a representative of the agency that referred them to therapy. They do not easily believe or trust that what they share in therapy will remain confidential and will not be used against them in the future. Hembree did identify the place where African American men do feel safe seeking help and guidance. The report states:

> African American men often find nontraditional counseling, however, with community kinship networks. For example, many men seek out family members or close and trusted friends for help with problem resolution or decision making. They may also seek the guidance of a minister or other religious leaders associated with the Black Church. In addition, (as it has already been mentioned), African American men have traditionally found non traditional counseling services in community centers of male social activity such as barbershops, taverns, or fraternal/social organizations. These are places where men engage in informal conversation and significant male bonding. Such centers allow men to informally, and often indirectly, discuss personal issues with trusted confidants in a non-threatening atmosphere.[7]

I disagree with the writer of the report referring to the organizations listed in the quote as being non-traditional counseling services. It is a cultural perspective that determines what is viewed as traditional or non-traditional. In

---

7. Ibid., p. 173.

the African American community these are the traditional places to seek help within the context of the culture.

THE NEED FOR TRAINING FOR CLERGY AND CHURCH LEADERS

There is a great need for training for clergy and church leaders about mental health issues. The lack of education and training leads to many misperceptions of the nature of mental health and counseling. In a report "Implications For Improved Pastoral Health Counseling" (Hyman & Wylie), research showed that persons often turn to the minister for help in a variety of health-related matters involving physical, mental, and social problems. These problems include alcohol abuse, illicit drug use, mental health problems, and sexual problems among all age groups. A conservative estimates indicates that over ten million persons in the United States are afflicted annually with Sexually Transmitted Diseases. Further this report points out that:

> Although the minister is in fact a sought-after health counselor he or she frequently lacks the technical and educational background in health counseling.[8]

The section of this research titled "The Minister as a Health Counselor" revealed the following:

> Many that are affected by these and other health problems search for help from various sources.

8. Bill Hyman, M. S., Wayne E. Wylie, ED. D., "Implications For Improved Pastoral Health Counseling" (Texas A & M University College of Education, Department of Health and Physical Education 1987), pp. 162–68.

> Some seek the help of physicians, while others look for help from mental health experts and professionals. However, research over the past two decades indicates that many people first turn to the minister for help. Gurin, Veroff, and Feld stated that 42 percent of the individuals who sought professional help for personal problems first approached the minister.[9]

Many people see the pastor as linked to God. The pastor is the mediator or intercessor for the people. This study cited several factors contributing to the minister's popularity as a counselor for various health problems. The minister is popular in the community because of their training and experience as a leader in the community, desire to serve, skill in personal visits and public speaking and the tradition for centuries of being the person to turn to for counseling in the parish and the community. This report also points out that in some cases there is a resistance to refer to professionals and gives some reasons:

> Clergy have been shown to be particularly effective in the counseling of adolescents. Greenspan and Fuchs reported that adolescents are often unreceptive to professional psychiatric help because of the distrust they have for this profession. However, ministers are more trusted by young people due to their position, the less formal setting, and the freedom from parental therapy monitoring.[10]

9. G. Gurin, J. Veroff & S. Feld, *Americans View Their Mental Health A Nationwide Interview Survey,* (New York, NY Wiley, 1960).

10. H. S. Greenspan, & A. D. Fuchs, "The Rabbi and The Psychiatrist Effective Counseling for Youth," *Journal of Religion and*

The quote above shows young people develop trusting relationship with their pastors over the years and because of this profound level of trust pastors are effective in counseling this group or if necessary make an appropriate referral to a professional counselor.

But this report also highlights that there is some clear resistance on the clergy's part to take on this important responsibility of counseling, at least for the clergy in the majority community. The clergy in the majority community expressed that they feel inadequately prepared to offer counsel in many areas:

> Wylie reported that over 50 percent of the ministers he surveyed indicated that they were not adequately prepared to offer counsel in many of these areas. Although they were most often called upon to offer marital counseling, 59 percent said they were not adequately prepared to do so, and in the fifth most popular area of counseling, mental and emotional health, 81 percent indicated that they were not adequately trained to counsel. The only area these ministers felt prepared to counsel were in spiritual and doctrinal matters. Wylie's findings supported earlier work of Greenspan and Fuchs who reported that ministers often felt inadequate to perform a variety of counseling services with their congregation and community.[11]

Health, 1978, Vol 42, pp. 4370A–4371A.

11. W. E. Wylie, "Health Counseling Competencies Needed By the Minister," *Journal of Religion and Health,* 1984, Vol. 23, No 3, pp 237–48.

Significance of the Problem of Resistance 23

However, this admission of feeling inadequate does not suggest that the clergy in the larger community would not take advantage of continuing educational opportunities that would further prepare them to meet some of the needs in their communities:

> Rogers reported that the 45 Baptist ministers he surveyed indicated a significant need for additional education or consultation in the areas of parenting, marriage, stress, single adult problems, referrals to mental health professionals, legal issues in counseling, depression and suicide, low self-esteem, divorce, and anger. According to Ruppert and Rogers most ministers would consider attending seminars designed to strengthen their counseling skills…These ministers also indicated a need for additional education in the areas of stress, marital communication, psychological testing, divorce, depression and suicide, pastoral stress, anger, delinquency, sexual difficulties, and working with mental health professionals.[12]

At the conclusion of this study, indirectly if not directly, it was clear by the recommendations of this report that congregations in the majority community, for the most part, did not expect the senior pastor to provide mental health counseling, although they still came to him or her first. Further it was recommended since many people still seek out the pastor, that a minister of health position be developed to take the pressure off of the senior pastor. This

12. P. P. Ruppert, & M. L. Rogers, "Needs Assessment in the Development of A Clergy Consultation Service A Key Informant Approach," *Journal of Psychology and Theology,* 1985, Vol. 13, No 1, pp. 50–60.

recommendation, to some degree, is a reflection of the congregation's resistance to being referred outside the church for their health needs, including mental health needs to be met. The position of minister of health would be similar to the positions of minister of finance, music, and religious education. As Cafferky suggested:

> This minister of health education would not only be responsible for the health counseling needs of the congregation, but also for other health related areas within the organizational structure of the church. Recreational and fitness or wellness programs are now becoming integrated into diverse environments, and the church is a prime setting for these types of programs.[13]

A survey of African American pastors in Southern California appeared in the *Journal of Pastoral Care and Counseling* in the Spring-Summer 2006 issue entitled, "African-American Clergy's Perception of the Leading Health Problems in Their Communities and Their Role in Supporting Parishioners' Health." One finding that stood out was the differences in White clergy and Black clergy concerning their perceived ability to provide counseling in several areas:

> It is the opinion of the pastors in the present study that mental illness is the result of a medical illness. Pastors held favorable attitudes toward the mentally ill while lacking in knowledge about mental illness in general. Researchers have found that clergy are generally confident in counseling

13. M. E. Cafferky, "Whole Health Education The Religious Workers Role," *Health Education*, 1982, Vol. 23, No 2, pp. 25–27.

across various mental health issues, except for severe mental illness issues, and are most confident in addressing spiritual, moral, and marriage and family issues. Clergy in The Church of Christ frequently counseled their parishioners in alcohol and drug abuse and severe emotional problems. Black clergy felt more confident than White counterparts to counsel people.[14]

This article also examined the practice of all clergy regarding referral and identified some of the barriers of the referral process. The clergy knew very little about the resources in the community regarding mental health providers compared to physicians and school counselors: "Researchers have found that although many people seeking help first approach clergy, less than 10% of those seeking help are referred to mental health professionals."[15]

In the Findings Chapter of this study the reader will see some of the same reasons for such a low referral percentage, such as the clergy's lack of knowledge of community mental health resources. Clergy do not refer parishioners to mental health professionals when moral or religious issues are the presenting problems. However, if the professional counselor is a Christian, then that is another factor that would determine if a referral would be made. In the mental health system clergy are called the "gate keepers." Therefore, one

14. Donnie W. West, Ph.D, "African-American Clergy's Perception of the Leading Health Problems in Their Communities and Their Role in Supporting Parishioner' Health" *The Journal of Pastoral Care & Counseling*, 2006, Vol. 60, p. 16.

15. Willa D. Meylink and Richard L. Forsuch, "Relationship between Clergy and Psychologists: The Empirical Data," *Journal of Psycholgy & Christianity*, 1988, Vol. 7, pp. 56–72.

factor that contributes to resistance of parishioners to seek professional counseling is the pastor's attitude about professional counselors. In a dissertation entitled "Attitudes of Fundamentalist Pastors toward the Causes and Treatment of Mental Illness," Cheryl R. Azlin states:

> A negative relationship was revealed between pastors' perceived competency in treating emotional disturbances and their attitudes toward mental health professionals and services; it appears that the greater the pastors' perceived competency to treat emotional disturbances, the less favorable were their attitudes toward mental health practitioners and services.[16]

Another noteworthy relationship to whether clergy would refer parishioners to mental health services was the size of the congregation. If the congregation was large, then the clergy were more likely to refer to mental health professionals. If the congregation was small, then this was not found to be the case. Therefore, one factor in whether referrals are made is clergy's time management. There may be other factors, such as education and class differences between many large and small congregations. Also, educated, middle-class families are more likely to use mental health services in both the White and African American communities. The study found that White clergy were more likely to prefer referrals to social workers, community mental health counselors, and physicians.

---

16. Cheryl R. Azlin, "Attitudes of Fundamentalist Pastors toward the Causes and Treatment of Mental Illness," *Dissertation Abstracts International*, 1993, Vol. 53, p. 4942.

There is limited research on Black clergy and referrals to mental health professionals. Bernard Richardson, Ph.D., Associate Professor of Counseling, Southern Connecticut State University conducted a study of 27 pastors and 81 parishioners in a Michigan city to measure attitudes of black clergy toward mental health professionals. The report is titled, "Attitudes of Black Clergy Toward Mental Health Professionals: Implications For Pastoral Care." The study assessed the attitudes of black clergy and their parishioners toward mental illness and mental health professionals. Although at one time black ministers were recognized as both religious and secular leaders in the black community, as well as having significant influence as a mental health interventionist, this is beginning to change with the development of comprehensive community mental health centers and psychological services there are alternative services. But whether or not a parishioner seeks the services from a mental health professional may depend largely on the attitudes the minister has toward mental illness and psychological services. The research cites Bentz and Edgerton whose work looked at rural communities and attitudes toward mental illness and leadership. The general public states:

> The leadership of a community may be a major factor in changing attitudes toward mental illness. Leaders, by virtue of their positions, exert a tremendous influence on social norms, and should be considered as playing an important part in the process of attitude formation and change. The general public tends to follow social standards established and articulated by the community's leaders. Thus leaders, through their

innovations and examples, can and do influence the attitudes of the general public toward mental illness.[17]

In regard to the African American community Dr. Richardson states:

> In view of the black minister's importance in the black community and the almost total lack of empirical data concerning this issue, it was therefore important to assess the attitudes of black ministers toward mental health professionals. A major assumption of this research was that the attitudes of the black pastors toward the mental health professionals would be unfavorable. This assumption was based partly on an observation that in the black community there appeared to be a negative stigma attached to persons who were under psychiatric care. It was therefore assumed that this negative stigma would also apply to mental health professionals. Another reason for assuming that the clergy held unfavorable attitudes was related to a popular notion that black ministers are losing their influence in the black community.[18]

The study included Baptist, Methodist, Church of God in Christ, Seventh Day Adventist, Pentecostal and Apostolic.

---

17. W. K. Bentz and J. W. Edgerton, "Consensus on Attitudes Toward Mental Illness Between Leaders and the General Public in a Rural Community," *Archives of General Psychiatry,* 1970, Vol 22, p. 468.

18. Bernard Lester Richardson, "The Attitudes of Black Clergy and Parishioners towards Mental Illness and Mental Health Professionals," *Dissertation Abstracts International,* 1982, Vol.43, p. 1192.

The majority of the churches had a membership of less than 100 members, and only five had over 400 members. The results were that black clergy had favorable attitudes toward all three categories of mental health professionals: psychiatrists, psychologists, and counselors. They regarded them as sincere, valuable, wise, safe and dependable. Parishioners were favorable towards these professionals but more favorable toward the clergy. There was no reason given for the positive attitude toward mental health professionals by both clergy and parishioners. However, it was suggested that, in this city in the state of Michigan, the availability of psychiatric services was widely known, which ultimately led to social acceptance. This result does not support the idea that black clergy have a sense of professional identity crisis in this city. An examination of clergy attitudes in other regions of the country should be reviewed to determine if this is true in general. According to Edward Wimberly:

> Slowly, black people have begun to look away from the church for leadership, because more and more black people are being educated and trained. Opportunities for black lay people outside the church have been lessening the influence of the black preacher. As a result of this new development, many pastors are in the midst of an identity crisis and need help in developing new skills of guiding.[19]

This one study did not substantiate that black preachers are losing their influence or that they are experiencing an identity crisis. It does appear that in the majority church

---

19. E. P. Wimberly, *Pastoral Care in the Black Church* (Nashville, TN Abingdon Press, 1979), p. 37.

clergy do not feel adequately trained in dealing with mental health related issues, but would take advantage of additional training in these areas. It is also apparent that ministers in some regions of the country have a great impact on whether parishioners resist accepting a referral to mental health professionals. However, there was not a clear definitive statement about whether parishioners actually follow through with referrals made by their pastors to mental health professionals. The literature did not address this important element of resistance in the larger faith community, although there has been some discussion on this subject in the African American community. The *Clinical Handbook of Pastoral Counseling* (Wicks, Parsons, and Capps 1985 p. 309) describes attitudes of African Americans toward counseling outside the family and church:

> Attitudes exist in the black community that may not facilitate the use of many models of counseling and therapy (Smith, 1981). For example, discussing family matters with outsiders is often considered a violation of family ethics. Personal problems are often carried to kinship members and especially to the mother. Moreover, general feeling exists that it is in church where one's deepest thoughts and emotional stresses should be addressed. Other attitudes hindering the use of counseling include not seeing the value of childhood experiences as the cause of poor mental health, viewing mental/illness as environmentally determined, and the rejection of the intrapsychic model of counseling and therapy (Smith, 1981). Often the role of the counselor is viewed as alien, and many do not see how counseling

> can help the fight for survival. Counselees (sic) want specific advice on matters and tend to see whites counselor as irrelevant to black contexts because of the menacing social and economic problems that black people face.[20]

Another important point regarding why African Americans have historically sought help from the pastor is that the black pastor was the smartest and most educated person in the black community.

Jason R. Curry's unpublished doctoral dissertation at Vanderbilt University (May, 2005) entitled *Exploring The Correspondence Between The Preferences of African-American Congregants and The Tenets of Prevalent Pastoral Theologians: A Metropolitan Study In Kentucky* states:

> The lack of research concerning African-American and pastoral care and pastoral counseling may be attributed to claims made by African-American scholars which suggest that African-American are reluctant to receive counseling in general. African-Americans scholars in the fields of psychology and religion have suggested that African-Americans are reluctant to receive counseling in a structured environment because of the following reasons: 1) a lack of trust between African-American counselees and white therapists, 2) the cost of therapy, 3) fear and/or distrust of system/institution by poor African-Americans, 4) the lack of interest by social science researchers, and 5) a cultural per-

---

20. Robert J. Wicks, Richard D. Parsons, Donald E. Capps, *Clinical Handbook of Pastoral Counseling* (New York, Paulist Press, 1985), p. 309.

spective which highlights the significance of the collective over the individual. In the summary written by Worthington et al. regarding Lyles' (1992) survey of seventeen African-American pastors, the authors maintain, "barriers to psychiatric referral included religious and racial concern, skepticism and psychiatric efficacy, and financial concerns.[21]

I believe that many of the reasons for resistance in the African American community to referral to professional counselors would also apply to working class and lower income white people in towns or rural geographic areas of the country. There are many isolated communities where people do not seek help for emotional and psychological issues from professionals, but instead turn to the clergy. Further research on resistance in the majority community should be conducted to better address this issue and to determine how to provide appropriate referrals. Additionally, many of the same reasons for resistance in the African American community may be seen in the majority community.

---

21. Jason Richard Curry was a doctoral student in the Graduate Department of Religion at Vanderbilt University who has completed a dissertation titled *Exploring The Correspondence Between The Preferences Of African-American Congregants And The Tenets Of Prevalent Pastoral Theologians: A Metropolitan Study In Kentucky*, May 2005, pp. 24–25.

3

Theological Perspective

IN THE African American church tradition, the pastor has always used the Holy Bible in teaching and counseling members. The Hebrew Bible has been a resource for pastoral counseling as many of the stories of the Hebrew Bible can be easily described to parallel the African American experience. One example is the Book of Job. The story of Job does not explain the mystery of suffering but it examines the depths of faith in the midst of suffering. The story of Job has been used many times in the pastor's study, counseling persons struggling with why the righteous must suffer. The Book of Psalms is also useful for the counseling pastor to gain insight into troubles and fears. The hymn writers provide hopes, aspirations, and reasons for confidence in the midst of tribulation. A verse from Psalms 30:5b (NRSV), "Weeping may linger for the nights, but joy comes with the morning," is a standard text for helping the distressed hold on for better times. These are a few examples of how the Bible's collection of Wisdom Literature (including Ecclesiastes and Proverbs) has and continues to be used in pastoral counseling. The pastor uses the scriptures to transmit the insights gathered in the tradition of the Israelite elders, as well as experience and observation. These particular books emphasize the process of moral formation: honesty, diligence, trustworthiness, the ability to hear or obey, control of one's appetites, the cultivation of true and proper speech, and the correct attitudes towards riches and poverty. Jesus' teachings to search one's own heart before judging others, such as Matthew 7:3 (NRSV) "Why do you see the speck in your neighbor's eye, but do not notice the log in your own eye?" or about serving two masters in Matthew 6:24 (NRSV), "No one can serve two masters; for a slave will either hate the one and love the other, or be devoted to the one and despise the other. You cannot serve God and wealth"; or Matthew 6:21, "For where your treasure is, there your heart will be also" are key texts that are relevant in a pastoral counseling context for African Americans.

In the New Testament Jesus uses a pastoral image in his call to bring comfort to the afflicted when he proclaimed in the synagogue in Nazareth on the Sabbath (Luke 4:18–19; (NRSV):

> The Spirit of the Lord is upon me, because he has anointed me to bring good news to the poor. He has sent me to proclaim release to the captives and recovery of sight to the blind, to let the oppressed go free, to proclaim the year of the Lord's favor.[1]

I believe Jesus was talking about one's emotional, mental, and spiritual well-being and being liberated from the demonic persecution one faces daily. Further, I believe

---

1. The Holy Bible NRSV Luke 4:18–19 (Nashville:Cokebury 1989), pp. 887–88.

Jesus was talking about more than one's physical being when he said in Mathew 11:28–30 (NRSV):

> Come to me, all you that are weary and are carrying heavy burdens and I will give you rest. Take my yoke upon you, and learn from me for I am gentle and humble in heart, and you will find rest for your souls. For my yoke is easy and my burden is light.[2]

One can argue that Nicodemus was in search of pastoral counseling when he came to Jesus by night. Nicodemus was in despair and spiritual crisis when he made his infamous visit in the secret of the night. In John's Gospel (John 3:5–6 (NRSV), Nicodemus went away from his session with the Great Counselor with a new freeing insight.

> Jesus answered, "Very truly, I tell you, no one can enter the kingdom of God without being born of water and the Spirit. What is born of the flesh is flesh, and what is born of the Spirit is spirit.[3]

Typically, African Americans have always thought the answers to their problems, whether external or internal, could be found in the pastor with his/her knowledge of what the "Good Book" has to say about their condition. In the eyes of many, there is no need to talk with anyone else. Many in the African American church believe "you take your problems to Jesus and leave them there."

The theological perspectives of the power of seeking help from the pastor can be seen in the works of Edward Wimberly (1990 pp.13–14) in his book, *Prayer in Pastoral*

2. Ibid., p. 841.
3. Ibid., p. 918.

Counseling Suffering, Healing and Discernment. Wimberly presents a "Discernment Model" for pastoral counseling using the narrative of Christianity. According to Wimberly:

> The discernment model draws on narrative language to express how the Spirit works at deep psychological levels in the lives of peoples. This means that the work of the Spirit can often be identified through the language of story. In the New Testament and the early church, as well as throughout the Old Testament, people sought to express God's presence in their lives by telling their stories of God's encounter with them. Through story they were able to help others see where God was working in them and to reinforce their own faith in the process.
>
> In the discernment model, the pastoral counselor seeks to help the counselees to discern God's story unfolding in their lives just as God's story unfolds in scripture. The counselor also assists the parishioners and counselees to bring their own stories into line with God's unfolding story.[4]

The discernment model categorized by Dr. Wimberly has always been in the Black Church, (thanks to Dr. Wimberly we now have a formal counseling model), and the pastor has always used the biblical narrative to help troubled people who sought their counsel. The pastor is the primary source for biblical interpretation for most African American parishioners.

---

4. Edward P. Wimberly, *Prayer in Pastoral Counseling Suffering, Healing and Discernment*, (Louisville: Westminster/John Knox Press 1990), pp. 13–14.

Theological Perspective 37

The historical perspectives of pastoral care can be traced back to the beginning of the early church. The only outlet for people in need of comfort and healing was the pastor. This is documented in the book, *Pastoral Care In Historical Perspective* (Clebsch and Jaekle 1983 p.13). I cite the following background information not as an argument for pastoral counseling being provided in the church but to show the key role the church has played in *the care of the soul*. Christian pastoral care can be traced back to A.D. 180, according to the work of Clebsch and Jaekle in their book, *Pastoral Care In Historical Perspective*. These two authors describe eight era or epochs of pastoral care that have always played a key role in the care of the soul in the church as an institution: 1) Primitive Christianity focuses on sustaining souls through life; and 2) Under Oppression was from A.D. 180-A.D. 306. This period was the reconciling of troubled people to God and codifying major sins and appropriate penalties. This was the legalistic period; 3) Christian Culture was when Emperor Constantine the Great made Christianity the official religion of the Roman Empire. The church guided persons to conform to the new Christian norms; 4) The Dark Ages was when care of souls was opposed by induced guidance; 5) Medieval Christendom or the Middle Ages involved the sacramental system being designed to provide guidance for the care of souls; 6) Renewal and Reform involved the rise of individualism in the Renaissance and Reformation which generated a great upheaval in doctrine and in ecclesiology that never became a revolution on the care of souls; 7) Enlightenment focused sharply upon sustaining souls in a wicked world; and 8) The Post Christendom Era (late 1800s and early 1990s) revolted against the Church of early times and brought pastoral work around guidance that taught values and norms from personal convictions and value systems.

Throughout its 2000 year history, the church has been the institution for pastoral care and counseling. In the African American community, tradition is very important because of the type of institutional slavery from which the Black Church was birthed. African Americans are a people who had language, culture, religion, and customs completely taken away from them. Therefore, when African Americans developed new traditions, religion, and customs during and after slavery, these elements of culture in the Black Church were very important. Moreover, since the Black Church has been the place of care, it is the first place people turn to for help and, as this study reveals, for some people, the only place. Spirituality in the African American community is grounded in scripture and in an active prayer life. Edward Wimberly (1994) developed a model for using scripture in counseling. He used the biblical narrative and the psychological narrative of the counselee to help bring healing. This model could be used in individual, marital and family counseling by using the Hebrew Bible and the narratives of the New Testament. According to Dr. Wimberly,

> All pastoral counseling begins with the presenting problem that individuals, marital partners, and families bring to pastoral counseling. The problem usually unfolds like a story, in dramatic fashion one scene at a time. Consequently, I spend the early stages of counseling attending to the presenting problem and the story that surrounds the problem. Once I have heard the

> story related to the presenting problem, I make an attempt to gain insight into how this story has developed over time and how it is related to the counselee's personal history, family history, relationship history, and other factors like education, health, vocation, and sexual functioning.[5]

According to this model the counselor can reveal the narrative picture the counselee has of their life. When the personal mythology is understood then the connection with the present problem can be made for the counselee. African American church goers, in many cases, learn the narrative stories in the Bible, and if they can relate their narrative to a narrative in the Bible it can help them see how to respond to a variety of personal situations in life and how they view God's presence or God's distance in the situation causing their presenting problem. The counselee is then requested to explore what they would want to result from the pastoral counseling experience, which is called the preferred story. The Bible can be used to help design the preferred story. Then the next step is exploring the person's life and the story that will be the focus of counseling. After this process has occurred goals can be set and the process of re-authoring the personal mythology and dealing with the presenting problem begins. Wimberly uses the re-authoring process to modify the personal mythology through pastoral counseling using the stories in the Bible.

I find Wimberly's model of narrative therapy using the scriptures to be beneficial for those persons coming to pastoral counseling when their faith tradition is a part of their

5. Edward P. Wimberly, *Using Scripture in Pastoral Counseling*, (Nashville, Abingdon Press: 1994), pp. 21–25.

daily life experience. In previous counseling experiences I have inquired about whether a counselee had a particular biblical character or biblical story they identified with in relationship to their presenting problem. Many people identify with the biblical characters or narratives and can directly relate to their situation. This information helps put the situation and the belief about how God is active in their life or distance and how they feel about their spirituality in perspective. A clergy counselee was unhappy about their denominational structure and how they were over qualified to serve in the church to which they were appointed and in a city they did not like. I asked what biblical character they identified with at that moment. After thinking about it for several moments the person said "Jonah, I feel like God spit me out in a place I do not want to be." In the following session the counselee talked about how using this image got them in touch with feelings of abandonment by God. We could then process those feelings of abandonment and what that meant for their willingness to serve that community.

The other element of the African American spirituality is an active prayer life. An appreciation and the assessment of this role in clients and their family of origin is very important in understanding their presenting problem. In working with African American families the technique of spiritual reframing can be useful. In the section on Spirituality and Therapy, Nancy Boyd-Franklin states:

> In the course of treatment, many African Americans will talk about their use of prayer to cope with life's challenges (Broman, 1996; Constantine et al., 2000). Broman (1996) found that this was particularly true for African

> American women, who use prayer to cope with health and mental health issues. Therapists should feel free to inquire about this use of prayer, and should even ask the client for examples of how she or he prays. I learned the importance of inquiring, rather than making assumptions, when treating a mother who was very distressed about her teenage son's drug use. She repeatedly reported in therapy that she prayed for her son. Most of her statements about him to me had been so negative that I decided to inquire about the words she used when she prayed for him. She replied, I pray "Dear Lord, please keep me from killing this child." Once I recovered from my surprise, I was able to reframe this by helping her to see the value of "positive prayer."[6]

There appears to be two schools of thought on the use of prayer in formal counseling sessions. I received two different answers from two different clinical directors at my training site regarding the appropriateness of the pastoral counselors praying with counselees. I was told it would not be appropriate by one director and it would be appropriate if the counselee requested prayer by a different director. I have experienced prayer being requested by both African Americans and white counselees. Again it depends on their spiritual reality and if prayer is an important part of their daily life.

In this chapter I have tried to explain how African Americans in particular need to see the problems and issues that are causing them distress in a religious context. I believe this is one of the main reasons they seek out the

6. Ibid., p. 127.

pastor for counseling first. Further, if they do not feel that a secular professional counselor, or for that matter a pastoral counselor, will be sensitive to their understanding of God and where God is in the midst of their problems, then it is going to be very difficult for the pastor to make a successful referral. I have attempted to emphasize the uniqueness of some African Americans' spirituality. There must be an appreciation of this uniqueness for those who attempt to refer these parishioners to a secular psychotherapist. One of the reasons why some African Americans will not take a referral to a secular psychotherapist might be the lack of understanding of the importance of African Americans' spirituality and that it must be integrated into the psychotherapy process. Further, this chapter provided evidence of the great need for more African American pastoral psychotherapist/counselors.

4

Methodology

PARTICIPANTS

THE INTERVIEWEES were drawn from the Tennessee Conference of the United Methodist Church which is comprised of seven districts. There are 52 African American churches in the conference with 4357 members, averaging 2603 in attendance during the time of this study. The Nashville District has 10 churches with 2401 members with an average attendance of 1231. The Murfreesboro District has 8 churches with 617 members, averaging 293 in attendance. The Cumberland District has 7 churches with 531 members, averaging 318 in attendance. The Cookeville District has 10 churches with 325 members, averaging 339 in attendance. The Clarksville District has 7 churches with 238 members, averaging 240 in attendance. The Columbia District has 6 churches with 184 members, averaging 141 in attendance. The Pulaski District has 4 churches with 61 members, averaging 41 in attendance. There are 32 charges served by 15 full time ministers and 17 part-time ministers. The 15 full time ministers include 10 ordained elders in full connection. The majority of this information was obtained from an unpublished document by the Tennessee Annual

Conference Black Methodists for Church Renewal, Inc. titled, "Strengthening the Black Church for the twenty-first Century" (1999–2000).

Six African American ordained elders in full connection were selected to participate in this research project. The size of their congregations ranged from 75 to 1,000 members. One of the criteria for the selection process was identifying those pastors who were known to do pastoral counseling. Another criteria was those who were known to refer parishioners to professional counselors. Because each annual conference within the United Methodist Church may require additional courses for ordination purposes, all participants were from the same conference. All participants have a Master of Divinity degree, but the number of pastoral care and counseling courses taken varied depending on the particular seminary from which each graduated. Three pastors were from a metropolitan area with one pastor having a large membership congregation, one pastor with a predominantly professional membership congregation, and one pastor with a small membership congregation. These pastors have over 20 years of experience each in the ministry. The last three pastors were from county seat churches in surrounding counties in Middle Tennessee. Their congregations have few professional congregants; congregational makeup was predominantly farmers, factory workers, and service industry workers. These pastors had 10 to 20 years of pastoral experience in a church. I had been acquainted with each participant on a professional level for several years. The participants did not appear guarded and spoke frankly.

Methodology 45

PROCEDURE

Participation in this project was strictly voluntary and confidential. Informed consent was a requirement. Names were changed to protect identities of pastors and persons who came for counseling. No participant was identified personally. Any identifying characteristics, such as location, age, gender, etc., were also changed in order to maintain confidentiality of persons who came for counseling. To further safe-guard the identity of participants and their parishioners, all completed surveys, forms, transcripts, audiotapes, and my journal were destroyed following the completion of the research project. The research proposal was reviewed and approved by the Human Subjects Review committee at Garrett-Evangelical Theological Seminary and follows the Code of Ethics of the American Association of Pastoral Counselors (See Attachments A & B).

The interviews took two weeks to schedule and complete, from August 15, 2007 through August 28, 2007. The length of time for each interview was 1 to 2 hours. All interviews were audio-taped and I kept a journal of each interview. Interviews were conducted either in the participant's office or my office. The data was obtained by asking the participants to 1) share two or three stories about individuals coming to them for pastoral counseling; 2) determine whether the pastoral counseling was sufficient; 3) whether they had made referral to an appropriately trained professional counselor in the community.

There were five categories of follow-up questions regarding participants' thoughts and observations regarding African Americans and counseling or referrals (See Attachment E).

Participants were debriefed after the interview and given assurances that confidentiality would be maintained. They were also informed that they would be given an opportunity to read the results of the research project after the study had been approved by the doctoral committee.

EVALUATION MEASURES

A mixed methodology of qualitative and quantitative analyses was used. Complete interviews, research and interviewees' narratives as well as figures are provided to support my hypothesis. Each participant received a briefing of the interview process: that a tape recorder was used to capture participants' stories, the tape recordings would be transcribed, and both the tape recordings and transcripts would be destroyed after the research project was completed. The Informed Consent form was signed by all participants.

The interview protocol was designed to identify the factors that participants believe help and hinder parishioners who come to them for counseling but do not seek additional help from qualified professionals within the community. The questionnaire gave each participant an opportunity to share narratives regarding their experience in providing counseling and/or making referrals (See Attachment E).

Five categories of follow-up questions were used depending on the response of these counseling stories. The total number of follow-up questions that could possibly be asked of participants were 21. During the six interviews not all follow-up questions were asked. Questions were open-ended in order to decrease "yes or no" answers. The five major questions were: 1) Why do you think people who seek counseling from the pastor will not accept a referral to a pastoral counselor or other counseling professional? 2) Why do you think some African American parishioners reject referrals to trained professional counselors? 3) Do African Americans view professional counseling as alien since families and churches deal with their inner personal concerns? 4) Do you define pastoral counseling as the act of receiving personal advice from your pastor, any pastor, or a member of the clergy inside or outside of the church? Why? 5) What professional counseling resources are available in your community?

CODING

Coding was accomplished by reading over the transcripts and listening to the audiotape of each interview several times to identify emerging themes. Coding was also accomplished by reading the journal I kept of each interview. The face-to-face interviews were transcribed by a professional with many years of experience in transcription. Once transcribed, the content was coded for themes related to the research questions and hypotheses. The transcript was 96 single spaced pages in length. The transcript was cross-referenced with the audio tape to capture the atmosphere during the interview. To protect confidentiality the counseling stories were modified if shared in the dissertation. I identified the common or important themes that surfaced during the interviews in Tables 1–4 in Chapter 5 entitled Findings. Consent was obtained from two participants to have their interviews included as attachments to the dissertation (See Attachments C & D).

QUALITATIVE ANALYSIS

The qualitative method of research was used because the data gathering approach allowed the interviewees to tell their stories of providing pastoral counseling in the local church, and to share their insight into why they were successful or not in attempting to make appropriate referrals to professional counselors. This method gave me the opportunity to share in their counseling experiences as I faced the same reality in my counseling experiences in the local church. Qualitative analysis is flexible in research design so I was not forced into a strict data gathering design. The pastors shared their experiences in their own words. Taylor and Bogdan state in their book, *Introduction to Qualitative Research Methods*:

> When we study people qualitatively, we get to know them personally and experience what they experience in their daily struggles in society. We learn about concepts such as beauty, pain, faith, suffering, frustration, and love, whose essence is lost through other research approaches.[1]

This form of data gathering was conversational and less formal in nature, which put the interviewees at ease. I believe they were able to freely share these experiences which were more insightful into what they experience as pastors and to what the people coming to them appeared to experience.

1. Steven J. Taylor & Robert Bogdan, *Introduction To Qualitative Research Methods*, (New York, John Wiley & Sons, Inc., 1998), p. 8.

In the research project, the African American pastors' descriptive observations of how and with whom parishioners share their sacred stories is very insightful. This method of research allows the clergy interviewed to share their realities from their point of view. Each of the six clergy who participated in the project were asked to reflect on parishioners who came to them for help and the social meaning each attached to their world as they shared their stories.

The strengths of the qualitative method of research were 1) this method provides data from people's own experiences, and 2) in their own words about a particular behavior or phenomenon. The method looked at patterns of data rather than collecting data. Through these patterns of data themes of resistance were identified, as displayed in the tables in Chapter 5. Another, strength of this method was an open dialogue whereby pastors were not required to give answers to a list of interview questions or fill out a questionnaire. They drew on their own experiences and observations from their place of praxis. Their counseling experiences allowed me to ask follow-up questions when appropriate. In regard to the limitations of the qualitative method I am aware that those who read this study might feel a larger sample group would have been preferable, I did not. The noted weaknesses of the research method were that most clergy are not use to sharing their stories and being audio taped. The process of transcription was difficult in some cases because a few pastors did not speak clearly into the tape recorder. The audio recording process may not have been comfortable for all participants, although every effort was made to assure participants that their interview would be confidential.

5

Findings

THE PURPOSE of this chapter is to better understand why many African American have a resistance to seeking mental health professionals and choose counseling with the pastor instead. The benefits of understanding this phenomenon include: 1) better training for pastors on the referral process; 2) developing a congregational based pastoral counseling system; 3) creating a heightening awareness that there is a great need for African American clergy to specialize in the ministry of pastoral counseling, all of which will promote healthier congregations. The value of using the qualitative research method and the procedure used in the interview process was discussed in Chapter 4, Methodology. This chapter presents a detailed summary of the interview experience with each participant. A qualitative approach to data collection and analysis was utilized. In this chapter, themes I identified with each participant and patterns are shared.

In the interviews, the six pastors shared 18 counseling stories about why the vast majority of parishioners resisted referrals to professional counselors in the community. Twelve factors or recurring themes were identified, as reasons parishioners did not go to a professional counselor either before or after seeking help from the pastor. They included: shame, family secrecy, economics, fear of being labeled "crazy," denial, guilt, lack of time, lack of trust, cultural insensitivity, pastor's attitude toward professional counselors, counseling was the pastor's job, and parishioners did not want to change their behavior. These recurring themes were separated into major and minor themes. A theme was considered major if three or more of the six participants had witnessed that reason parishioners came to them for help, but would not go to a professional counselor. A theme was minor if two or fewer of the six participants had witnessed that reason parishioners came to them for help, but would not go to a professional counselor. The following tables list all themes, recurring themes, major themes, and minor themes.

ALL THEMES FROM INTERVIEWS ABOUT WHY PARISHIONERS RESIST REFERRALS
TABLE 1

	Shame	Family Secrecy	Economics	Label "crazy" Stigma
Pastor #1	X	X	X	X
Pastor #2	X		X	
Pastor #3			X	X
Pastor#4	X		X	X
Pastor#5	X	X	X	X
Pastor#6	X		X	X

The results of the interviews with the six participants as shown in Table 1 identified twelve possible themes regarding why parishioners would resist referrals to professional counselors. Participants stated they had observed eleven of the twelve themes listed in the tables in parishioners who came for counseling. The one theme that did not get cited was "the pastor's attitude toward professional counselors."

	Do not want to Change Behavior	Denial	Guilt	Pastor's Job
Pastor #1	X		X	X	X
Pastor #2	X	X	X	X
Pastor #3	X			X
Pastor #4	X	X		X
Pastor #5	X	X	X	X
Pastor #6				X

	Lack of Time	Pastor's Attitudes toward Professional Counselors	Lack of Trust	Cultural Insensitivity
Pastor #1	X		X	X
Pastor #2				X
Pastor #3				
Pastor #4			X	X
Pastor #5	X			X
Pastor #6			X	X

PASTOR 1:

... we as African Americans I've discovered are very secretive. We don't even tell our own family stuff. So, indeed I would say, we as African Americans, we need someone else other than the pastor to counsel with. Because we have so many stigmas about our sharing self and we want to share stuff and get it out of our system but we want to share with somebody we don't see on a regular basis and we know they are not going to see any our friends or family members. So when it comes to African Americans, I really feel like because of the fears and underlying currents of mistrust that the African Americans definitely need someone other than the pastor to confide in.

Interviewer:
That's interesting because basically this research project is looking at why African Americans will come to the pastor but will not go to an outside professional for help. So has your experience been that African Americans tend not to bring those sacred stories to the pastor. Do you think they take them to outside professional counselors or do you think they just keep them in the family and keep them a secret?

Pastor 1:
For the most part, I think they try to keep them in the family and keep them secret. As I alluded to a moment ago, it depends on the level of relationship that you have. I've had in some of the places I've pastored, persons who felt like I was family and they would share the family's dirt with me knowing that, hey, I am not going to share it with anybody. And then there are other persons in that same congregation, who never got close enough to me to let me know their middle name. You know. So it depends on the level of comfort that the person is at and the level of professionalism that the pastor has.

Interviewer:
Okay. On the African American parishioners rejecting referrals to trained pastoral counselors or trained counselors, I just have a couple of questions I want you to answer. To what degree do you think shame plays when parishioners refuse a referral to a professional counselor, like in the case of the woman with the handicapped daughter. Do you think shame had any thing to do with her not seeking help?

PASTOR 1:
I'm sure there was some shame there because even though I was in their apartment for almost four years, I never found out who the father was of the child, and, I mean it was always hush, hush. I believe shame was a big part in it as well as her denial.

Interviewer:
Denial of the handicapping condition? What role do you think economic status plays in coming to the pastor for help versus going somewhere else? I think you already touched on that a little bit.

PASTOR 1:
Yeah, Yeah, Well, they feel "we're paying him for something, so let's get all we can out of him." (laughter).

Interviewer:
I just have a few other follow-up questions just to get your thoughts on. Do you feel that African Americans think that it's the pastor's responsibility for their mental, emotional and spiritual needs?

PASTOR 2:
Yes,

Interviewer:
Why?

PASTOR 2:
The pastor has been in the African American church; the pastor has been all of that. And we as African Americans, until recently, haven't had access to professional counseling or a psychiatrist. That has just recently come about and so still; you don't have enough professional counselors that's out there for African American so all of that is put on their pastor.

Interviewer:
Okay. Have you ever experienced anyone refusing a referral?

PASTOR 2:
Yes, on a few occasions.

Interviewer:
Do you think shame had anything to do with it?

PASTOR 2:
Yes, it had a lot to do with some, probably cost, and some was very resentful and upset with me for referring them to the counselor.

Interviewer:
Do you think that African Americans view professional counseling, outside of the pastor, but a professional counselor either a pastoral counselor or either a psychologist or somebody like that? Do you think that the majority of African Americans view that alien to them, since the family and the church deal with their inner personal problems. Or they think that the family and the church should be the place that they take their problems?

Pastor 3:

I suppose they think the family and the church should be the place they take the problems. Also, in small communities, where everybody knows everybody Black and White.

Interviewer:
Huh!

Pastor 3:

People don't want to become stigmatized. As being mentally ill or mentally deficient or, crazy. And, huh, so I think that's another one of the reasons why African Americans doesn't (sic) seek professional help outside the pastor and the church.

Interviewer:
Do you think that it's the pastor's responsibility to provide not only for their spiritual needs but for their emotional needs and mental health needs also?

Pastor 3:
In many ways, I think so. I really think so,

Interviewer:
Do you have any idea why? Is it traditional, or is just that they see the pastor as God's representative and the pastor would know, how to help?

Pastor 3:

I think perhaps that's a big part of it. See the pastor, as God's representative and pastor will know how to help. Yet I think they come to every situation with their preconceived notion of what the pastor should do. And if the pastor is not leaning in the direction that they feel like the pastor should be leaning, then perhaps the pastor is not helping them.

Interviewer:
But for church members, if they sort of incorporate the pastor into the family and then its like keeping whatever the issues are still in the family by talking to the pastor would that be what you meant by seeing it as an extension to the family?

Pastor 3:
Yes,

Interviewer:
That theme has come up before.

Pastor 3:
Has it?

Interviewer:
Yes, and I was just checking you to see if you felt that too?

Pastor 3:
But one of the things I try to stress is that we are a family. We are family and we treat and love one another as a family.

Interviewer:
Do you think that, people who come to the pastor see the pastor with issues that are something that maybe considered secrets that only people in the family know about that are issues that they are dealing with? Do you think that they come to the pastor because not only do they see the pastor as God's representative but they also see the pastor as an extension of the family? Or do you think that doesn't have anything to do with it?

Pastor 4:

I see that many see the pastor as God sent and as an extension of their family. Case in point, I have pastored a person, who was a mental health professional. Who would invariably come by and say "Rev., let's go to lunch." He would take us to lunch so he could talk about his problems. But, ah, I find that most people need someone, an outside source, to vent their frustrations to and some of us will go to a psychiatrist, some of us will go to the preacher, or a trusted friend or a family member. So it's very difficult. But I was really surprised that this individual being a trained professional that he felt like he had a need to talk about personal things in his life. He felt like he could come to his preacher. He felt rather secure, why he would come to his pastor.

Interviewer:
Probably would. Do you think that African Americans feel that white counselors do not understand them? Are not culturally sensitive to them and they have a problem going? And if qualified African American pastoral counselors were available do you think more parishioners you've needed to refer would go to them or just go to someone else?

Pastor 4:

Yes, Most definitely. Cause, when I've had to make referrals, first thing they would ask me, "Is he African American?"

Interviewer:
Do you think that if an African American pastoral counselor is trained in a white training environment, the African Americans will see him/her as viewing their situation with the same insensitivity of a white counselor?

Pastor 4:
Oh, No.

Interviewer:
What degree does shame play in the role of refusing a referral?

Pastor 4:
I think it plays a big part? I think that's why many people refuse to go. They are ashamed. People look at a psychologist or a psychiatrist will tell them whether they're sane or not sane and need help.

Interviewer:
Do you believe that economics play a role and huh?

Pastor 4:
Most definitely.

Interviewer:
Them coming to pastors for help versus professionals?

Pastor 4:
Oh, they'll call the pastor before they go, Yes! Economics.

Interviewer:
Tell me do you think, I mean to your knowledge, did this lady call the person that you referred her to? Did she get additional counseling?

Pastor 5:
Well, I actually referred her to you.

Interviewer:
No she didn't call me. Do you have any idea why she didn't call?

Pastor 5:
If she went to anybody else?

Interviewer:
Anybody else or if not, why do you think she didn't follow through with your referral?

Pastor 5:
Okay, my guess is that she didn't. Huh, my sense is that most people don't want to deal with the question of going to a counselor. There is something wrong with that. I'm not, that means I'm crazy? Part of it though for some people is their concerns about cost. And that's one of the things that I can say to them is that, in terms of where you (referring to the interviewer) are, there is a sliding scale based on income that is very helpful in terms of people who are struggling with being able to cover that. And now I am really pushing more toward putting it in our church budget to give something financially to the counseling center, not a whole lot, but something, it's a start. You know that we can continue to refer people, so that this service can be available in that way for them. (Interviewer: Huh, huh.) So to deter any concerns people may have about, well I can't afford it. Yeah, that may be a piece of, but I think the other part of it is that people are afraid, afraid, of that even people know that I've been to counseling and they'll think something is wrong with me. I think fear also, and I can speak this even for myself and my own experience afraid of getting in touch with the pain. Not wanting to go there. (Interviewer: Right). If they're comfortable believing that I can't go there, then they may keep coming to me, you know, but she (Pastor 5 is referring to herself) can only go so far. But when I refer them to you

or someone like you, who can go deeper. There's a fear of getting in touch with that pain again and not wanting to go there even though to go there may be just the thing they need in order to begin their healing process and that's part of what I try to convince people of; and then sometimes sharing my own story of my own hesitation at one time about counseling. Is that ooh, you know, I understand that it's hard to go there but I promise you, you really need to go there and it would help. But I think that's part of it to. Sometimes people just don't want to go that far, all right. And then for some people it's that they got a million and one thing going on and don't see that as a priority because of all of the other responsibilities, like this lady I was just telling you about. You know she's helping to raise her sister's children, her mother was diagnosed with a major illness recently. She's got a wealth of things on her shoulders and I try to talk to her about taking care of herself. But she doesn't understand the value of taking care of herself and doing it for those that need for her to be healthy, emotionally and psychologically and spiritually. So that she can be, be more effective, in taking care of those other people that she is trying to look after. This is something that I think is true with many women we tend to put our needs behind the needs of other people.

Interviewer:

Do you think African Americans, in general, view professional counselors as alien since the family and the church deal with the inner personal concerns in our community?

PASTOR 5:
Alien to the church? Well, I mean I think?

Interviewer:
No, alien to them because they believe that the church and the family is where you take your inner personal issues?

Pastor 5:
So, it's not an option? Is that what you are saying?

Interviewer:
Yeah, yeah, they wouldn't choose professional counseling as an option or they would rather keep it within the family or take it to the pastor?

Pastor 5:
Ah, I guess that's true.

Interviewer:
Do you have any idea why?

Pastor 5:
I think that we spiritualize it too. This whole thing of "If you just take it to Jesus, what do you need a counselor for? You just need to be able to pray and take it to Jesus and just you know. And let him have it and he'll heal you, he'll take care of it. He will straighten it out." That is I think a mindset of many African Americans within the church, that if they just pray about it, you know, you don't need no counseling. But if you do think you need to talk to somebody, but then they think "I don't know if you can trust that pastor." (Laughing). You know. (Laughing). (Interviewer Huh, huh!) But the thing is, but the real thing, I think many times is to keep it within the family. Keep it quiet. "You don't need to tell our business. You don't need to put our business out in the street. The pastor don't even need to know our business,

don't nobody need to know, keep it here!" Okay and I think that's the mindset that makes counseling a non option. Just don't even think about. "I don't need that." Yeah. This is our thing. Or it's either keep it within the family. You know, "we don't tell our family business. We can handle our stuff. Or, lets just pray about it, God will do it. You know you don't need all that stuff." And, some preachers preach that.

Interviewer:
Do you think African Americans think it is the pastor's responsibility to provide for their mental, emotional and spiritual needs?

Pastor 5:
Some people do. This lady I just talked to on the phone last night, (laughter), yeah, last night, kept me on the phone for three hours. I kept trying to find a way off the phone. And one of her statements that she made was, "she told somebody that you can call the pastor any time of day and night. That's what the pastor is there for. Whenever you need the pastor, just call her. That's why she's there. I know she's got her family and stuff." She's telling me this (laughter). (Interviewer Chuckle.)

Interviewer:
Do you think African Americans believe white counselors would not be understanding or culturally sensitive?

Pastor 5:
Huh, yes.

Interviewer:
You think that's the reason that they will not take referrals?

Pastor 5:
Referrals to white counselors?

Interviewer:
Huh, huh.

Pastor 5:
Yeah, definitely. I do, I do. Because, ah, you know, cause there's a lot of difference in terms culturally how we are raised in the African American community versus a white community and I think a lot of times there this assumption just because we're all human, and we're all Americans or whatever or we're all Christians or whatever, or whomever you may be. That we're just made alike and it justs not that way. But, a lot of times the cultural environment which we are raised really impacts, ah, interpretation of things and I see a lot when I'm in meetings and you know, I see how we interpret, some of us interpret the very same thing, but come out with a very different perspective on it. You know its because of what has informed us culturally, where our experience as a culture that defines how we interpret the situation. So, if you're coming from a totally different culture, cultural experiences in American culture is not just a big soup, its not all the same. You know we've got a lot different cultures within the American culture. So if you come here with this culture and you're imposing that mindset onto my situation.

Pastor 6:
People come to the pastor because they really don't want to be labeled, but they realize that you know they want their problems addressed. They want to be able to leave that ses-

sion without having someone to label, or to be given medication that further labels them. So I think that the pastor offers opportunity for people to find some rescue, and some restoration.

Interviewer:
Now in the case of the woman addicted to drugs or her husband who is also addicted to drug? Are you talking about, in the case of his denial?

PASTOR 6:
Well, actually, in this particular case, that's a good question. I'm really dealing with her. Because I think that right now, he is still in the manipulative mode, he's not wanting help. He's in a position to get help. He's still very much insane, the kind of insanity that comes with crack and cocaine.

Interviewer:
Okay, could you tell me a little bit about the church in Ohio that actually started a pastoral counseling ministry?

PASTOR 6:
Okay, this church was in the heart of the ghetto in 1970, this was on the heels of the big riots. We found ourselves in a situation where we just pressed the issues and it was a lot of people in that community with mental health issues, but you couldn't get them to go out to these newly opened community mental health centers.

Interviewer:
Right.

Pastor 6:

And the notion came up this lady who was over the mental health center downtown, I was asking her for her assistance on how to get people, members of my church, people who I knew needed help and how could we get them help. She said, they need to come here and the fact of the matter is we started trying to get people to go and they wouldn't go. But at our church we always had a lot of people there, because we had a hunger program there, we had a thrift shop, we had two daycare centers. We had a lot of things going on, some activities were always there and it was not unusual seeing people going in and out of the church all day long, all day even into the night. So it became a natural that people didn't mind coming into the church no one in the community would see that as a stigma and so we developed a pastoral counseling ministry with trained counselors. They were social workers. It was not at a place with a big mental health sign and they were just going to church.

RECURRING THEMES OF RESISTANCE TO REFERRALS
TABLE 2

Themes	# of Pastors
Economics	6 out of 6
Pastor's job	6 out of 6
Label "crazy" Stigma	5 out of 6
Do not want to change behavior	5 out of 6
Shame	5 out of 6
Cultural insensitivity	5 out of 6
Denial	4 out of 6
Guilt	3 out of 6
Lack of Trust	3 out of 6
Lack of Time	2 out of 6
Family Secrecy	2 out of 6

Table 2 identifies eleven themes recurs in every participant's experience regarding resistance to referrals to professional counselors: Economics and Counseling as the Pastor's job was observed by 100% of the participants: Label "crazy" Stigma, Do not want to change behavior, Shame, and Cultural insensitivity was observed by 90% of the participants; Denial was observed by 60% of the participants and Guilt and Lack of Trust by 50% of the participants and Lack of Time and Secrecy less than 40%.

MAJOR THEMES OF RESISTANCE TO REFERRALS
TABLE 3

Themes	# of Pastors
Economics	6 out of 6
Pastor's job	6 out of 6
Label "crazy" Stigma	5 out of 6
Do not want to change behavior	5 out of 6
Shame	5 out of 6
Cultural insensitivity	5 out of 6
Denial	4 out of 6
Guilt	3 out of 6
Lack of Time	3 out of 6

Table 3 identifies nine major themes participant's experience regarding resistance to referrals to professional counselors: Economics and Counseling as the Pastor's job was observed by 100% of the participants: Label "crazy" Stigma, Do not want to change behavior, Shame, and Cultural insensitivity was observed by 90% of the participants; Denial was observed by 60% of the participants and Guilt and Lack of Trust by 50% of the participants.

MINOR THEMES OF RESISTANCE TO REFERRALS
TABLE 4

Themes	# of Pastors
Lack of Time	2 out of 6
Family Secrecy	2 out of 6

Table 4 shows only two themes: Lack of Time and Family Secrecy was observed by only two out of the six participants.

Secrecy can be very tricky to detect. The two women I referred to in chapter 1 came to me needing help processing being victims of incest in their childhood. They both had told their mothers what was happening to them. Their mothers did not believe them and took great effort to tell them they were lying. There was evidence of shame and guilt but I came to realize that the controlling power within those family systems was secrecy.

*It is important to note not one participant stated the pastor's attitude toward professional counselors was a cause of resistance to referrals from their experience.

C. Eric Lincoln and Lawrence H. Mamiya's book, The Black Church in the African American Experience (1990) lists the percentages of Black urban clergy who have various ministerial functions. Counseling ranks sixth out of nine responsibilities:"

> The results in table II show that for the black urban clergy, the task of preaching far outranks

> any other, 919 (60.0 percent). Second and third places, respectively, included teaching, 358 (23.4 percent), and church administration, 62 (4.0 percent). Fourth place was leadership of groups within the church 38 (2.5 percent). Fifth place was leading worship 22 (1.4 percent). There was a tie for sixth place visitation and counseling 14 (0.9 percent) and civic leadership 14 (0.9 percent). Fund-raising was seventh place 3 (0.2%) and no response 101 (6.7 percent).[1]

Because counseling has such a low rating, it may indicate that the emotional and mental needs of parishioners are not being met, and perhaps cannot be met by pastors with various levels of training.

---

1. C. Eric Lincoln and Lawrence H. Mamiya, *The Black Church in the African American Experience* (Duke University Press 1990) p. 136.

TABLE 5

Participants	Years of Experience	Membership	Churches Served
Pastor #1	26	305	12
Pastor #2	32	1019	7
Pastor #3	11	100	8
Pastor #4	46	79	13
Pastor #5	16	340	2
Pastor #6	35	346	4

The data in this table was obtained from the Tennessee Annual Conference 2006 Journal. This data shows the six participants in this research study have a combined 166 years of experience in pastoring churches.

SUMMARY OF FINDINGS

The results of the interviews with the six participants, as shown in Table 1, identified twelve possible themes regarding why parishioners would resist referrals to professional counselors. Participants stated that they had observed eleven of the twelve themes listed in the tables in parishioners who came for counseling. The one theme that did not get cited was "the pastor's attitude toward professional counselors." It is important to mention that one pastor did state, in one case, there was a therapist he would not refer to again because of a bad working experience, but he would refer to other professional counselors in the future. All participants, but one, felt inadequate to provide pastoral counseling beyond brief crisis counseling or pre-marital counseling. The one pastor who identified himself as a pastoral counselor is known in the community as a pastor who does pastoral counseling. He states his training for pastoral counseling comes by pastoral "experience." Also he has some addition training in counseling through continuing education and a practicum working at an institution providing pastoral counseling while attending seminary. In this case the finding cited in Chapter 2 regarding the larger the congregation the more frequently parishioners were referred to professional counselors was the opposite in this pastor's approach. In the present study the pastor of the largest congregation provided more counseling on a regular basis than did the other five pastors interviewed.

The results displayed in Tables 2 and 3 regarding the major themes of resistance to referrals to professional counselors by parishioners were not surprising such as: 1) economics; 2) providing counseling is the pastor's job; 3) being labeled "crazy" or stigma; 4) cultural insensitivity by white counseling professionals ; 5) shame; 6) parishioners do not want to change their behavior so they come to the pastor because there is no accountability requiring change; 7) guilt; and 8) Lack of trust in professional counselors. The surprise was the low percentage of participants who had not observed family secrecy as being an issue in resisting sharing their stories. Nancy Boyd-Franklin states that secrecy is a major motivator in resistance within the African American community. While only two pastors listed this as something they observed I wonder if secrecy was not a key element in the shame that five of the six participants saw in parishioners who came to them for help. The interviews confirmed the concern African Americans have regarding being labeled "crazy" or having the stigma of being mentally ill attached to them by going to a professional counselors, 5 out of 6 participants observed this concern in parishioners. The matter of not having the time to seek help from a professional counselor by parishioners being low was not surprising it is another form of resistance.

As seen in Table 2, economics was observed by all participants as a major barrier to seeking professional counseling. This seemed to correlate with the finding that parishioners believed that meeting their emotional and mental needs was part of the pastor's job. This is a major issue since all participants, but one, felt they did not have the time or training to provide an effective ministry in this important area. All participants felt they were not trained to provide the level of counseling for the problems with which they had been confronted in the local church from their seminary courses; although one participant had received addition training and one participant had a unit of Clinical Pastoral Education (CPE). The pastors' reluctance to counsel because of their lack of training is a positive sign. These pastors are not trying to do more than they are trained to do. There are several themes that surfaced in this study that were also identified in Chapter 2 on Resistance. Other African American studies identified the themes of racism, fear of being labeled "crazy", and family secrets, these were found in Nancy Boyd-Franklin's research. Secrecy was also found in Emma Justes work with older women. Cultural insensitivity and lack of trust was discussed in Daniel Hembree's study.

There are several other comments made by participants that are worthy of mention.

Pastor #1 observed the secretiveness in the African American community and even within the family system secrets are withheld from some family members. But if the family views the pastor as part of the extended family they will share their secrets with the pastor. He observed there is a need to share some family secrets with someone they trust and someone they do not see regularly. When the level of the relationship evolves to viewing the pastor as part of the family the fear of the stigmas of mental illness decreases because they believe the pastor will not share the family secrets with anyone.

Pastor #2 is known for his counseling skills and counseling people from other congregations. He has people traveling from other parts of the state for pre-marital counseling. This pastor sees himself as a professional counselor. His observation is that people want concrete advice from the pastor. This pastor saw lack of accountability as a motivator to seeking counseling from the pastor. The pastor does not have the official authority of the professional counselor. Further, if the parishioner wants to they can choose non-compliance with any treatment goals established in pastor/parishioner counseling sessions. Therefore the parishioners can continue their inappropriate behavior if they wish.

Pastor # 3 was very familiar with the resources provided in the small town she served and made appropriate referrals. This participant was also aware of the law requiring notification to the appropriate authority of potential damage or threat to a person's life and safety. This participant was the only pastor to observe in the setting she served as pastor that African Americans would not have a problem being referred to a white professional counselor and would prefer a white counselor more so than a black professional counselor.

Pastor #4 compared the parishioners of African descent from the Caribbean to African Americans and found that people from the Caribbean appeared to revere their pastors more and looked forward to talking to their pastor about almost any incident that happened in their lives. Their commitment to the church appeared to be stronger than with African Americans. This pastor also observed that parishioners saw their pastor as God's representative and an extension of their family. He further noted that rural church people are different than city people out of necessity. Because many times in the African American United Methodist rural congregations the pastor is not a resident minister in the community, but travels to the community on weekends and as needed, there is usually a patriarch in the community that seems to have more influence on the congregation. This patriarch would be the person parishioners would take their problems to more so than the pastor.

Pastor #5 refers to herself as a pastor who counsels and not a pastoral counselor, although she had some courses in counseling in seminary and a unit of Clinical Pastoral Education (CPE). She sets a limited number of times she meets with a person and then after making an assessment she refers to a professional counselor. Her willingness to refer is related to her training. She is able to do some diagnosis of the parishioners and knows her limitations. She assumes the parishioners follow through with the referrals and makes the appointments with the counselor. This pastor sets appropriate boundaries for parishioners when it comes to developing friendships. In some cases she provides some form of spiritual directions for persons coming to see her for spiritual matters. She has observed that African Americans take many emotional or psychological issues to the pastor because African Americans "spiritualize" problems that come up in life. They have been taught to "just take it to Jesus, what do you need a counselor for." Many African Americans believe in praying and taking it to Jesus and many do not know if they can trust the pastor.

Pastor # 6 refers to himself as a pastoral conversationalist more so than a counselor. This pastor has observed that many African Americans resist professional counseling because of the labeling and being prescribed medication as further labeling. He started a pastoral counseling center in a church and it works very well. People did not have to worry about being seen going to a pastoral counseling center and being labeled. The church operated several services to the community and people were always going in and out of the church. This pastor had observed over his years of experience that many pastors try to meet all kinds of expectations of parishioners and others, causing a negative impact on the pastors. As the participant stated, "when pastors try to meet all the needs people presented to them they burn-out or self destruct" because there were no boundary lines of where their responsibility ends and another professional's responsibility begins. Some pastors don't know where their responsibilities stop. Fortunately this same participant has witnessed the younger generation realizing that there are other options for them and they have the finances to obtain these services from professionals other than the pastor.

There were no new themes that came from the interviews with pastors that were not mentioned in Chapter 2 on resistance. Although the participants for the research project did not reveal negative attitudes toward professional counseling, further research regarding the attitudes of a larger sample of African American clergy would be helpful.

6

Conclusion

MY HYPOTHESIS in this research project was that African American parishioners resist counseling from professional counselors for two reasons: a) a history of racism and cultural insensitivity in the mental health system; and b) a lack of education and training by African American pastors and church leaders.

The psychological and theological literature cited in this study supports this hypothesis. In Nancy Boyd-Franklin's book, *Black Families in Therapy: Understanding the African American Experience,* effectively proves that racism is the cause of many of the issues facing African Americans seeking help beyond the family and pastor. After seeking therapy, many African Americans are fearful that they will be labeled as "crazy." African American families are often not self-referred, meaning that some social welfare agency or other public entities such as schools, courts, or hospitals have sent them for treatment under pressure. The African American community has a negative history of the welfare system and other social agencies going beyond their legal boundaries into the private business of the family. Another reason for resistance by African American families is the perception that the family must keep "family secrets" private. In his doctoral dissertation (2003), *Person, Community and Divinity in Yoruba Religious Thought and Culture: Foundations for Pastoral Theology With African American Men,* Daniel Troy Hembree quotes from the American Counseling Association's report on resistance in African American men. The resistant attitude about counseling may be a defense mechanism among African American males because they generally view counseling as an activity conducted by agents of a system that has rendered them virtually powerless. This is another view of the system taking away their manhood. Secondly, further examination to address the problem of silent suffering in the pews is realizing pastors need additional training in pastoral counseling.

Interviews with six pastors showed that there were eleven reasons why African American parishioners resist referral to professional counselors: 1) economics; 2) pastor's job; 3) label "crazy" stigma; 4) do not want to change behavior; 5) shame; 6) cultural insensitivity; 7) denial; 8) lack of trust; 9) guilt 10) lack of time; and 11) family secrecy. I believe that, based on these observations and pastoral experiences of six elders in the Tennessee Conference of the United Methodist Church, the hypotheses of this study have been proven. Although I will admit this was a small sample of pastors, these six pastors have a combined 166 years of experience in the ministry. Two of the six pastors have experience pastoring churches in other regions of the United States. I believe my methodology of a qualitative study was appropriate for this kind of study. A qualitative methodology allows the investigator to collect data using people's own observations and experiences.

I was surprised to learn that secrecy was a theme for resistance because it can and is disguised in the other major themes such as guilt, shame, economics, lack of empathy, and lack of trust. The study also showed the amount of re-educating pastors and parishioners need in order to direct particular needs in the congregation to qualified professionals. In my discussion I have shown how some of the reasons for resistance are related to the racism and cultural insensitivity of the mental health system, while other reasons are related to the misperceptions and lack of training of pastors. When the pastor believes he/she is responsible for meeting the needs of their congregants when some needs are beyond their scope of practice they too are shackled by a heavy burden.

IMPLICATION FOR FUTURE RESEARCH—A NEW MODEL OF PRAXIS

I have concluded from this study that there is a need for pastoral counseling and training services that are more accessible and more sensitive to the needs of African American parishioners. One model would propose partnerships between local congregations and pastoral counseling agencies to provide pastoral counseling services to African American parishioners and to provide training for African American clergy. This model could potentially address both sides of the problem—lack of sensitive and accessible services and lack of training of clergy. This model would be a congregational-based counseling paradigm that fills the void between the church and the pastoral counseling center. The mental health community bears some responsibility for their history of racism and cultural insensitivity. I mentioned this historical relationship in Chapter 2 under the section Racism Within Mental Health Theories, Practices, and System. This model would be designed whereby the pastoral counseling center would take their services to the consumer in the safety of their church facilities. Joel K. Fairbanks, PhD gives one example of a congregational-based counseling paradigm. Fairbanks states in an article in the *American Journal of Pastoral Counseling* (Vol. 3(2) 2000), entitled, *Integration of Counseling Services Within the Church: Development of a Church Assistance Plan,* that there is a model emerging that is similar to the Employee Assistance Plans (EAPs) called the Church Assistance Plans (CAPs).

> The CAP program would provide a church with a certain number of free, or discounted, counseling sessions for each church member at an established annual cost based upon church membership . . . Four Sundays were picked during the preceding year and the average attendance on those four Sundays was proposed as the contracted number of "church members." Also the cost of the program was initially staggering to most churches approached. Initially we proposed the 10% rule as applied by most EAPs, that is we calculated that 10% of the members would utilize three counseling sessions per year. We then calculated $50 fee utilizing three counseling sessions per year. We then calculated $50 fee per session to arrive at the project cost for the provider. Dividing the projected cost by church membership resulted in annual cost of

> $16 per church member. For example, a church with 300 members would be assessed an annual cost of $3,200, to be paid on a quarterly basis. However a church with 3,000 members would pay $32,000 per year. A wide variety of feedback was provided indicating that the churches wanted other options. An adjustable rate was then developed that would establish a co-pay by members receiving counseling services. Each $5 increment in co-pay resulted in a $2 reduction in rate per church member. So a church could still offer free counseling services at an annual rate of $16 per church member or offer counseling services which require the member to make a $5 to $25 co-pay and lower the annual contracted cost to the church. For example, a church may require a $15 co-pay for each counseling service and the churches contracted rate would drop to $10 per member.[1]

Although the model described above addresses the economics, I believe it would also address the other main themes of resistance: stigma, shame, cultural insensitivity, guilt, lack of trust, and secrecy. This model could be adjusted for small membership churches whereby churches within a 5 to 10 mile radius could develop one plan that would include all the churches to share the cost. This partnership model should be further researched and tested with several congregations and pastoral counseling centers to see if it is effective.

1. Joel K. Fairbank, "Integration of Counseling Services Within the Church: Development of a Church Assistance Plan," *American Journal of Pastoral Counseling,* Vol. 3(2) 2000, pp. 43–47.

IMPLICATION FOR ADDITIONAL CLERGY TRAINING ON MAKING REFERRALS

Another approach could be to better train pastors on making referrals. Many pastors do not know how to make an appropriate referral. They do not understand the importance of following-up with the parishioners to see whether they made the appointment and went to see the counseling professional. A successful referral is more than recommending that a person seek help from a professional. Since the literature in the study strongly supported the pastor is the first professional persons come to for help, pastors need the skills to assess whether the person wants to maintain their present lifestyle behavior or change. If the person shows no sign of their willingness to change, then a referral would not be helpful. Clergy may have to wait until persons are ready to make the necessary changes in their lives before making the referral. Pastors may also set a number of counseling sessions with a parishioner, and then make the referral. This would avoid the time commitment from the pastor and the dual relationship wherein the pastor is therapist and pastor to the parishioner, as well as the transference that may come from a therapeutic relationship.

Pastors should learn that there are several steps to a successful referral: 1) have an existing relationship with the professional they are referring to, make a point of not just finding a therapist or center to refer to but know the therapist; and 2) the pastor continues to meet a few times with the parishioner to ensure that they do not feel abandoned, and more importantly to ensure the parishioner is actually seeing the therapist for counseling. This additional training will limit the pastoral counseling sessions the pastor offers and be more effective in making appropriate referrals.

In conclusion the reasons many African Americans seek help from the pastor for their emotional and mental health needs have been outlined clearly in the Findings Chapter. The approaches to address this problem are threefold; 1) more training for pastors, 2) providing counseling services in the local churches by professional pastoral counselors, with one example of a method to pay for this service, and 3) train pastors there is a process to making an effective referral to a professional counselor which includes meeting with the parishioner after the referral is made.

In evaluating the methodology I used for this study I feel that the qualitative model was the best method. I believe I selected a very good representation of the pastors who agreed to participate in the study. I was impressed with the type of situations with which they are confronted in their daily ministry. Consistency with follow-up questions could have been better confronted. This report could benefit from the inclusion of clearer examples involved in dual relationships. I felt that in some interviews I could have gotten more information if I was more consistent with asking the same follow-up questions of everyone. I found myself getting focused on the various stories and may have been distracted from the informal interviewer role.

Implications for future research could include a study of pastors from other denominations, ethnic groups, and the majority community regarding this phenomenon of resistance to referral to professional counselors, and whether parishioners in these populations have similar reasons for resistance as were found in this study. The potential benefits could result in training pastors on the process of making successful referrals to professional counselors, pastors seeking limited supportive pastoral counseling training, developing a congregational based pastoral counseling system, promoting healthy congregations, and heightening awareness that there is a great need for African American ordained clergy to look into the specialized ministry of pastoral counseling.

The mental and emotional health of the people who sit in the pews and the clergy who stand behind the scared desk proclaiming the Word of God need the necessary tools to nurture not only their souls, but their mental, emotional and physical health. Then we can be free to grow into the church God is calling us to become no longer shackled by a heavy burden.

Appendix A

Letter Informing District Superintendents of the Research Project

Dear District Superintendent:

I am in the process of gathering research for my Doctor of Ministry Degree at Garrett – Evangelical Theological Seminary. I am conducting my research from 4 to 6 elders appointed to dominantly African American congregations in the Tennessee Annual Conference.

The focus of my research is why many African Americans choose to seek help for their mental health needs from the pastor and will not take a referral by their pastor to professional counselors. All parishioners' and pastors' identities will be kept concealed. The title of my research project is *Shackled by a Heavy Burden: An Examination of Barriers Pastors Face when Providing Pastoral Counseling or Referrals in the African American Church.*

This research will include:

- Potential benefit to the parishioners of African American churches and their pastors, as well as rural churches in obtaining needed pastoral counseling from trained professional.

- Potential benefit for pastor of referring the parishioners to congregational based pastoral counseling or

obtaining further training in providing limited supportive pastoral counseling.
- Potential benefits as the United Methodist Church seeks to have healthy congregations.
- Potential benefits for The United Methodist Church from the heightened awareness that there is a great need for African American ordained clergy to look into the specialized ministry of pastoral counseling.

There may be a slight risk to participants of the Investigator not recording their thoughts accurately. Parishioners whose stories will be shared by the pastor are also at risk of their confidentiality being breached. In an effort to reduce the risk of confidentiality breached, pastors will agree to protect the identity of the congregant's counseling stories by signing the form agreeing to participate in this study. A statement regarding protecting parishioner's confidentiality is in that agreement. Pastor's responses to interview questions will be kept confidential. Pastors will be asked if they are familiar with confidentiality as it relates to their pastoral relationship with parishioners. If they do not know it will be noted in the study. The investigator will explain what confidentiality means in relationship to this study. Persons in the congregation who sought counseling from the pastor will not be identified personally in any reports or publications resulting from this project. Any identifying characteristics will also be modified. Pastors will be directed not to use real names or any identifying information, when possible the circumstances in the stories may be changed to protect the identity of the person the pastor is sharing information about. The important information from the investigator's perspective is if the pastor felt able to provide counseling, if not why, and if they referred to a professional counselor and later follow-up with the congregant.

The participant's responses to the interview questions will be kept confidential. Participants will not be identified personally in any reports or publications resulting from this project. Any identifying characteristics will also be modified. The pastor's participation in the project is voluntary, and they may withdraw participation at any time by calling Rev. Murray with no negative consequences.

The interview will be taped for transcription purposes. At the conclusion of the project, all tapes and transcripts will be destroyed. All participants, the bishop, and cabinet will have the opportunity to see the dissertation after it has been submitted and approved for the Doctor of Ministry degree.

>If you have any questions please call me at 615–473–3482. You may e-mail me at Kmu52316@aol.com.

>Sincerely,
>Rev. Kennard Murray
>Seay Hubbard UMC
>1116 First Ave. South
>Nashville, TN 37210

Appendix B

Dear Pastor:

Thank you for your participation in this project. The interview process continues the research for Rev. Kennard Murray's Doctoral project titled, *Shackled by a Heavy Burden: An Examination of Barriers Pastors Face when Providing Pastoral Counseling or Referrals in the African American Church.* The project is in partial fulfillment of the Doctor of Ministry degree from Garrett-Evangelical Theological Seminary in Evanston, Illinois.

This project will engage participants in their experience as pastors when parishioners come to them for counseling for their emotional and psychological problems. The primary interview question will be for you to share two or three stories about individuals coming to you for pastoral counseling and whether you were able to help them or referred them to an appropriate trained professional counselor in the community. All parishioners' identities will be kept confidential.

Your responses to the interview questions will be kept confidential. Participants will not be identified personally in any reports or publications resulting from this project. Any identifying characteristics will also be modified. Your participation in the project is voluntary, and you may withdraw participation at any time by calling Rev. Murray will no negative consequences.

The interview will be taped for transcription purposes. At the conclusion of the project, all tapes and transcripts will be destroyed. All participants will have the opportunity to see the dissertation after it has been submitted and approved for the Doctor of Ministry degree.

By signing below, you give permission for Rev. Kennard Murray to use your responses to the interview questions for research purposes in the project and any future publications. Also you are agreeing to protect the identity of the person(s) you are sharing your counseling stories about.

Please make a copy for your files and return this form in the enclosed self-addressed envelope.

Participant's Signature_____
Date_____

Thank you again for consenting to be a participant in this research project.

Sincerely,

Rev. Kennard Murray
Seay Hubbard UMC
1116 First Ave. South
Nashville, TN 37210

Appendix C

Dear Pastor:

Again thank you for your participation in my research project titled, *Shackled by a Heavy Burden: An Examination of Barriers Pastors Face when Providing Pastoral Counseling or Referrals in the African American Church.* In order to enhance the dissertation I would like to use your interview as an attachment.

All parishioners' identities will be kept confidential as well as your identity. By signing below, you give permission for Rev. Kennard Murray to use your interview transcript as an attachment to the doctoral dissertation. Also you have received a copy of the interview transcript and approved its content.

Participant's Signature_____
Date_____

Appendix D

PASTOR 1:
August 15, 2007 Interview with Pastor 1

Interviewer:
Basically, Pastor 1, What I'd like for you to do is to share two or three stories about individuals coming to you for pastoral counseling and whether or not you were able to help them or refer them to an appropriate trained counseling professional in the community. And, if they resisted the referral to a professional counselor, what do you believe was the reasons for their resistance. Please do not use real names and if their circumstances appear to be very distinctive, we will change the circumstance before the report is written.

PASTOR 1:
Well, I had a bi-racial couple come to me and I (huh) mainly around children issues, because he had children from another situation and there were situations dealing with his not being up to date on his child support. I tried to get them to understand how difficult that situation was and that there needed to be a mediator between him and the mother of the children. For them to have counseling and everything, but they resisted and would not go. Then a month later, the wife came to me and shared with me that he had been incarcerated. So, that's one situation that could

have been alleviated had they went ahead and got a mediator and talked with the other party. Another situation I would share with you would be around the death of a member, that had no children, and when the wife died, all these nieces and cousins came out of the woodwork to help this man. I tried to get him to, well at that point to get legal aid, attorney or whatever to work with him. Because I felt that what was needed, but also he also needed some psychological help, because he and his wife had been married for 45 years and no children, so they really depended very heavily upon one another. And, as I said, these nieces and nephews came out of the woodwork and they began worrying him constantly about who was going to get what and so forth. So it really became agonizing for him and would have been good if he could have gotten away and had someone to help him to deal with his grief. Because they did not give him a chance to get over his grief, they were there with their greed trying to get what he had. So it wasn't three months, and then he expired. So our situations in our churches, our people need professional help because the pastors just do not have the time. Everyone is coming at different angles from him or her to help resolve their issues. "Would you like another one?"

Interviewer:
Sure!

Pastor 1:
Well, this young lady, she had a daughter, that was kind of handicapped and when I got assigned to the church, this young lady's mother, became like a surrogate mother to me, so I became kind of like part of the family in some regards.

Appendix D   97

And I spent a lot of time with them and tried to help her with the daughter, whose handicapped. The main thing I tried to do, I tried to get her to get social assistance for the child, but she was in denial about her child's handicapping condition and so she would not seek the kind of help the child could have gotten. So as time went on, "a single woman, preacher," people began saying that we were dating or whatever, even though we were like you know, sister and brother, basically this was the relationship we had and so because of that kind of communication beginning to develop, I started to remove myself, from you know the kind of contact I had in the past with the family. And, the child never did receive the kind of help that she needed and I guess, she is 16 or 17 now and I have no idea of where she is or what she is doing. But, I know that there is no way that she could have been productive in the school system with the condition that she had.

Interviewer:
Well okay. All right! In the first case, about the bi-racial couple why do you think that they resisted counseling?

Pastor 1:
I think they resisted counseling because, she had two children also, that were not by him. I feel they resisted because they did not want to reveal or become vulnerable by revealing themselves totally like that. Because they had been together, 11 year from what they shared with me and her youngest child was 13. So he has been with her, helping her raise her children, but he wasn't doing nothing for his own. I think that kind of feeling of guilt or whatever, might

have been something that prevented them from seeking counseling.

Interviewer:
Why do you think that they brought the story to you?

Pastor 1:
They brought it to me because I had initially given them some financial help to get their lights back on at the house where they lived. And I guess by sharing with me, they felt, you know, that it wouldn't go any further. It would be confidential and they could continue using me as a sympathy card so to speak and I'd keep on giving them the money.

Interviewer:
Huh, huh. So, it was more out of their financial situation that they came to you for help more so then advice or counsel.

Pastor 1:
No, they did not want counsel. They just wanted money! They just wanted me to help them pay the bills that they were spending their money on alcohol and they want me to pay their necessities. (Subtle laughter).

Interviewer:
Did you refer them to arbitrator, or counselor, or did you just tell they needed to find one?

Pastor 1:
I told them that I would help to get one if they wanted to. Huh, but that conversation just died.

Interviewer:
Okay, then in case #2, regarding the death of the wife and they had been married for 45 years and you felt that the husband probably needed some psychological help. Could you tell me a little about what made you think that?

Pastor 1:
Well, what made me feel that was because he had not had a chance to deal with his grief. Having experienced the death of my parents and my oldest son, I know there is a time where you want to be by yourself, there's a time where you want to cry, there's a time you want to share what you have had happened to you with somebody. He never had those opportunities. These people were there like vultures! They came in instantly, can I do this for you. But, in the same breath, they had a hidden agenda. They were wanting things. They were spying out the house. Seeing what in the house they could get. So this man never had a chance to really grieve.

Interviewer:
Okay. Do you think if those relatives hadn't came out of the woodwork, would you have been able to help him through their grief?

Pastor 1:
I think me along with some other person. I would have referred him to somebody else. Like I said, they had been together for 45 years. He would need someone older than me that he could really relate to, I think. Because they came through the Depression together, and all those other hard times and so he would really need someone, who could re-

ally relate to him after having come through all those other issues of life and still have some purpose for living.

Interviewer:
In the pastoral counseling field, there is a term that they use called "dual relationship," where they say that if you are a person's pastor, that you shouldn't be their counselor also. Because of that "dual relationship" that people might have some type of transference towards you good or bad or you might have counter-transferences towards them either good or bad. Or that you might incorporate some of what they have shared with you in a sermon or something like that. What are your thoughts on this term of "dual relationship?" Do you think that that is appropriate and that pastors shouldn't do counseling?

PASTOR 1:
This is a tricky one. I will answer the best way I can. I've been blessed to have served both races. When I was with the Caucasian churches it didn't matter
I did not use those kinds of stories and sharing in my sermons and that is very important. It's very hard for some pastors to draw that line but if you can draw that line then good but if you can't then hey, you shouldn't counsel you should just preach and teach and whatever. It does present a problem because people want to also be their pastor's friend and vice versa. And so, there are some things that you will share with a friend but there are other things you won't share with a friend because you want that friendship to remain strong. So, depending on the level of comfort a person has and the level of professionalism the pastor has, I would say that some counseling can be done by the pastor.

The pastor has to be able to be professional, has to know how to keep things confidential, if not, then he should stay out of it. When I came to the African American Church, we as African Americans I've discovered are very secretive. We don't even tell our own family stuff. So, indeed I would say, we as African Americans, we need someone else other than the pastor to counsel with. Because we have so many stigmas about our sharing self and we want to share stuff and get it out of our system but we want to share with somebody we don't see on a regular basis and we know they are not going to see any of friends or family members. So when it comes to African Americans, I really feel like because of the fears and underlying currents of mistrust that the African-Americans definitely need someone other than the pastor to confide in.

Interviewer:
That's interesting because basically this research project is looking at why African Americans will come to the pastor but will not go to an outside professional for help. So is it your experience that African-Americans tend not to bring those sacred stories to the pastor. Do you think they take them to outside professional counselors or do you think they just keep them in the family and keep them a secret?

Pastor 1:
For the most part, I think they try to keep them in the family and keep them secret. As I alluded to a moment ago, it depends on the level of relationship that you have. I've had in some of the places I've pastored, persons who felt like I was family and they would share the family's dirt with me knowing that, hey, I am not going to share it with anybody.

And then there are other persons in that same congregation, who never got close enough to me to let me know their middle name. You know. So it depends on the level of comfort that the person is at and the level of professionalism that the pastor has.

Interviewer:
Being a pastor, if you had any issues would you seek counseling from a professional counselor or would you seek it from another clergy person?

Pastor 1:
It depends on what it is. Now if it was something dealing with my own mental stability, I think I would talk to another clergy person. But, if it was something dealing with a relationship like my wife and I, a professional counselor. You know. I feel like I would go to a fellow clergy if there were some emotional problems I'm having related to my job, where as if it were something relational, huh! I would go to a professional.

Interviewer:
Why do you make the distinction about something emotional with yourself you would go to another clergy? Is that because another clergy might be able to identify better with those issues or what?

Pastor 1:
Yes, I feel they would empathize with me and understand where I am coming from more so than a professional person, counselor, who has never pastored or was not an African-American pastor.

Interviewer:
What about a pastoral counselor, who is located in a pastoral counseling center but previously have had some experience pastoring a local church, would you feel just as comfortable going to that person as you would another clergy or not?

PASTOR 1:
I would feel more comfortable with that person because I feel that this person has both dynamics that person has the dynamics of experience of pastoring and now they have been equipped with the psychological tools to help me deal with those issues that arise from me trying to be a pastor. One of the papers I wrote for my undergraduate degree dealt with pastoral burnout and it was amazing to find the number of articles I found where pastors had taken all they could take and were contemplating suicide. So, you know that field of pastoral counseling I can see it as being one that is very relevant and very needful.

Interviewer:
I would like to ask you a few follow-up questions based on the three stories that you gave me. They are sort of general questions. 1) Do you think men or women are more receptive to counseling and why?

PASTOR 1:
Women are more receptive because women are more open and women want to talk. Where as a man feels like nobody can tell him anything and we can fix it ourselves.

Interviewer:
Okay! And as far as making referrals, who do you think will take a referral quicker. A man or a woman?

Pastor 1:
A woman would. As I said, a woman wants to express herself and sometimes if it is a husband and a wife, e.g., the wife knows that the husband tunes her out, so she wants that third party, so that makes sure that the husband is listening. Where as we as men, the male characteristic is that you can't tell me nothing. (laughter).

Interviewer:
In what cases would you provide counseling? I know earlier you said, based on the pastor's time, there is so little time to do regular responsibilities, weekly long term or short-term counseling. Is there any cases where you would provide counseling or is it most cases you would refer?

Pastor 1:
Really, the only counseling that I do is marriage counseling and I have a set of videos and books that I use for that purpose and that is a basic thing. When it gets down into the dynamics of emotional and psychological make-up, I really think a person needs someone with more expertise.

Interviewer:
What program do you use for marriage counseling?

Pastor 1:
It's a program entitled, Making Marriage Work by, Les and Leslie Perrone.

Interviewer:
Do you think that African-Americans review professional counseling as alien to the family since the family and the church deals with the inner personal concerns? What do you think were the reasons in any of the situations that you just talked about no body actually went to a professional? Do you think it is because in the African-American community we really don't view professional counseling as being part of what we do?

PASTOR 1:
That's true and also some of the persons also especially the first story and the latter story think about economics. Whether or not they can afford somebody to do that and then the time issue. About the older gentlemen, time was no problem; money was no issue either, but just the fact that he was bombarded by people constantly. He didn't have the thinking ability to seek out help.

Interviewer:
Do you think during your training in seminary you were prepared to do counseling in the local church?

PASTOR 1:
I had three courses and the only course that really helped me any I feel was my field study. When I spent some time at a halfway house for young men. All of these men had a little handicap but yet they were at the halfway house not because of drugs but because of the mental handicap and they were making the transition into the mainstream of society but they needed that continuity of that home. The counselors were there to help them make sense out of what had happened that day so that they wouldn't have to keep it

on their minds and explode the next day. You know. In that one setting I don't think it was adequate because the human emotions cover such a wide gamut. There are so many possibilities and things that can trigger people and someone who has been trained to understand the psychology and the emotions and the fact that some people do need to be medicated for lack of a better term or either need to be in a facility where they can receive the kind of ongoing help that they need from someone whose been trained needs to be available to make that call.

Interviewer:
Do you feel that African-Americans think that the pastor's responsibility is to provide for their mental, emotional and spiritual needs?

Pastor 1:
In the African-American Church I feel. No, I only feel like that the pastor should help them in their spiritual needs.

Interviewer:
And, likewise, do you feel that the pastor has a responsibility for their emotional and mental needs?

Pastor 1:
I feel the pastor does have some responsibility but he can only have that responsibility to the degree that the people are willing to include you in their life.

Interviewer:
Do you feel that African Americans basically would rather have advice from their pastor rather than counseling? You

know, if they come to you with a problem, they would rather you give them advice about what they need to do?

PASTOR 1:

To answer that, Yes! they prefer advice and the way that many of them have come to me is that they have a friend. This friend needs this and their relationship, whatever. They come from that standpoint, rather than saying Pastor, it's me, I need advice about this, I need advice about that, they always use a friend.

Interviewer:

Especially in case number 1, may be in all three cases that you shared with me. Do you feel like the reluctance to take that referral, besides money and time, was that they felt like they would be going to a White counselor, professional and they didn't feel like that they would get the same understanding of what they got from you.

PASTOR 1:

A very good question. I'm really not sure. Could you read that question again!

Interviewer:

Do you feel like in the three cases, in particular the first two cases I know that you said that time and money, had something to do with them not taking a referral or seeking professional help from outside the pastor. But do you think that they felt that they would be going to a White professional and that White professional might not have the same empathy or understanding about where they are coming from and their experience and that might affect them resisting the referral.

Pastor 1:

That too might be a part of it, I think the greater part was time and finances.

Interviewer:

Do you think African Americans, basically reject the idea that whatever went on in their childhood could manifest in their adult life and so they really don't pay attention to the idea about going back and visiting your childhood to see what the problems they might be experiencing now might have started back then?

Pastor 1:

For the most part, I feel that our people, African-Americans are living in the day and for the day and don't want to think about the past. So that anything that might help that would come from reviewing of the past, they negate it. Because they're just in the here and the now. In the present.

Interviewer:

Do you think African-Americans pastoral counselors, if there are qualifying pastoral counselors would you refer people to them?

Pastor 1:
Yes, I would.

Interviewer:

Okay. On the African-American parishioners rejecting referrals to trained pastoral counselors or trained counselors, I just have a couple of questions I want you to ask about that.

To what degree to you think shame plays in the role of refusing, like in the case with the woman with the handicap daughter. Do you think shame had anything to do with her not seeking help?

PASTOR 1:
I'm sure there was some shame there because even though I was in their apartment for almost four years, I never found out who the father was of the child, and, I mean it was always hush, hush. I believe shame was a big part in it as well as her denial.

Interviewer:
Denial of the handicapping condition? What role do you think economic status plays in coming to the pastor for help versus going somewhere else? I think you already touched on that a little bit.

PASTOR 1:
Yeah, Yeah, Well, they feel "we're paying him for something, so let's get all we can out of him. (laughter).

Interviewer:
And do you think that the parishioners believe that the pastor is God's representative and will know how to help them so there is no need to seek help outside the pastor. Do you think that's a fair statement at this point?

PASTOR 1:
That would be true of the generation that is from 60 to 80, but the people who are below that age bracket. They see the preacher just as someone who helps them with their spiritual needs. I don't think they really see the preacher

as God's representative. Nor do they seem to feel like the preacher has all the answers.

Interviewer:
Okay. Do you define the pastoral counseling as an act of receiving personal advice from your pastor? Or not?

PASTOR 1:
If I did not have the level of training I have, then I would see it as that. But because I have the level of training I have and because I've had 26 years of experience pastoring. I know that is not what pastoral counseling is…

Interviewer:
How would define pastoral counseling?

PASTOR 1:
I would define pastoral counseling as the task of someone who has been trained in both the pastoral skills as well as clinical skills that are needed to help persons dig deep and find the underlying causes for their pain and grief to help them have fruitful lives.

Interviewer:
Are you aware of any pastoral counseling resources here in the community you serve in?

PASTOR 1:
I'm now becoming aware. I think the young man I'm with right now is in that field, but other than that, huh, I do know that there is a counseling center over on West End or Harding, whichever the road changes to. But as far as African -American counselor, pastoral counselor I think

the young man I'm with right now is the first one that I know of.

Interviewer:
In your church location do you get any homeless people or any street people in your area to come knocking on the door? Wanting money or just to talk or anything like that?

Pastor 1:
We are in the suburb, we are in a hidden corner. Even people who are coming there on purpose we got to give them maps. (laughter) So, we have no one coming there like that except when we have hosted Room in the Inn and then we will go pick up the guys and then we will bring them just for a meal and then there are persons who will open up and talk with us. But they are not looking for any real help; they just want someone to talk to.

Interviewer:
You will not see them again most likely.

Pastor 1:
Right.

Interviewer:
Okay, if you do not have anything else to share, thank you.

Pastor 2:
August 20, 2007 at 10:05 .am.

Interviewer:
Pastor I'd like for you to share two or three stories where you provided pastoral counseling to people who came to you from

the church or either from the streets and they needed counseling. If not, could you tell me about a couple of situations where you referred people to professional counselors.

Pastor 2:

Okay, one is I had a young man by the name of J., who came to talk to me last year. He was involved in an adulterous relationship with a member of the church. The young lady's husband at the time was away on his job for an extended period of time. He was actually one of the husband's best friends. The husband entrusted his three children to this brother J. He wanted to make sure they had a man figure because he trusted him and in turn, J. ended up going with the man's wife. Their relationship lasted the entire time he was away. When he got home the man found several letters about her relationship with J. They went through a rocky road. J. had come in for counseling. I was able to counsel him. I was able to share with him biblical principles, but more than biblical principles real life principles and trust principles. As far as what his friend was expecting of him. And how he allowed his guards to come down and the relationship began. Also, I shared, it was a vulnerable time for the young lady because her husband was away and J. began to come around more and more. She started looking at him differently and so their relationship began. I did counsel her and I counseled the husband. The husband and the wife are still together. J. moved out of the relationship and has another girlfriend he dates. The husband is working in another state. So, I am concerned again about that family and their relationship. Because he is in another state working to make a better life for his family and she is here with the three children. I have not counseled her or talked with her on that matter. I have talked with her a lot on other matters, but not how she's coping with her husband being away. I am somewhat concerned because, you know, huh? I think that she may still be somewhat vulnerable, but I'm hoping that she is not, but I haven't counseled her this time.

Secondly, I had opportunity to share with her husband, this brought ease to him. So he was able to cope with the relationship. We also had a 12-week counseling session with the husband and the wife to bring healing in their relationship and try to regain trust. So, I think that did happen. They seem more together because of their relationship. I knew some of the issues as to why she would seek other opportunities. He was not as attentive as she wanted him to be. Sexual practices were not on one accord. She liked certain things and he just liked one thing. So, that was a major issue in their relationship. We were able to talk through a lot of those issues. But I do think that at the end, they were together and J. had moved on. But as I said before, he is back in another state now and so I don't know what the situation is.

Interviewer:

Before, we go to any other case. Twelve weeks, how did you with all the duties of being pastor, how were you able to work in 12 weeks of counseling with this couple. Did you have other members in the church that you were providing pastoral counseling to?

Pastor 2:

I actually set aside a day a week for counseling. I found myself counseling church members at my church and other churches' members, especially larger churches, where the pastor is not available so I'm doing a lot of counseling for members of those churches. I'm a doing a lot of wedding counseling, but I am setting aside a time and adjusting my schedule so I can do it. There's also a time especially during pre-marital counseling, I have a format that people go through, so I have some other folk that kind of help me in that area. So that takes a little of the burden off of me.

Interviewer:
Do you feel like, the counseling with this couple and J. was successful? First of all, did you see your counseling with J. as more a religious issue; as far as committing fornication or adultery, I don't know if he was married or not? Did you see that more as sin or did you see it as type of flaw in his personality, where he was more of a predator? Huh, how did you view him?

Pastor 2:
I did not view him as a predator; I viewed it as he saw an opportunity and viewed her as very vulnerable, because of no one else being there to relate to her. So, I think the attraction was probably there, but I think it was an opportunity for him to be involved in this relationship.

Interviewer:
When you provided marriage counseling for the couple, in J's, case was the husband aware that you were aware of the relationship with the young man?

Appendix D 115

Pastor 2:
Right, matter of fact, he did. He knew that I was aware of everything.

Interviewer:
Okay.

Pastor 2:
And Ah,

Interviewer:
So how were you able to mend that broken trust through pastoral counseling?

Pastor 2:
Ah, I feel that one of the first things I did was meet with her on two occasions without her husband. I met with him on two occasions without the wife. Because, I think you have to understand and give people freedom to talk. A lot of people want to get couples there together; you do not get the truth from that. You have to have an opportunity where people can freely talk and so, being able to freely talk with each individual, I was able to ascertain the actual concerns that each had and also, I was able to put together some of the issues that would have been hidden had we been together.

Interviewer:
Okay, as far as the counseling, you felt like it was successful.

Pastor 2:
I think it was very successful. The only problem I do have is that I was not expecting him to leave for another year in a short-term, before the trust and relationship was fully con-

nected. I think it was fully connected, but I think, you had a person gone for a year, and so within that year, there was turmoil so six months they were having peace and healing and then six months later, he's gone again for a year. You know I'm waiting to see some of the results when he comes back. Obviously, they are going to need some counseling.

Interviewer:
As far as their issues in the bedroom, their sexual preference, how were you able to help them work through those?

Pastor 2:
One of the things I think myself, more than other counselors, I'm more real than most people. I know a lot of people, who want to rush around the issues, I ask direct questions. Because, if you don't ask direct questions, if you're trying to beat around the bush and if you're trying to just deal with what's not real, then you are not going to find out what the issues are, so I ask direct questions and I ask questions that people would call uncomfortable.

Interviewer:
Huh,

Pastor 2:
But if I'm going to help a couple, I need to know. I need to know what type of sex you have at home and I'm not afraid to ask that question. I want to know, if you like oral sex and I would ask them that. I want to know do you like freaky sex and what does that mean? I want to know every detail. I've had many letters from couples that I've counseled several over the past, I get letters all the time of thank you, they said,

I'm the most real person they have ever talked to. Because, if a person's sex life is not happy, they are certainly going to do some huh, there are possibilities of stepping out.

Interviewer:
Okay. Are there any other stories that you want to share?

Pastor 2:
Yes, there is, but I need a break. One second.
Yes, another case, huh, I had, huh, a young man by the name of X., to come in and we talked. His problem was drugs. It was extensive drug use, but he was a good dude and I felt he could be helped. I just felt I wasn't the person to help him. So I helped him as much as I could, I didn't give up on him and we did counsel him on about two occasions, but I felt he needed more detailed counseling and so I sent him to W's Professional Counseling Service.

Interviewer:
Is that a professional drug rehabilitation program? Or is that a private practitioner.

Pastor 2:
He's a private practitioner.

Interviewer:
Okay, but he has been trained in A&D treatment

Pastor 2:
Drug rehab?

Interviewer:
Were you able to follow up and see if the person went to the referral?

Pastor 2:
The person actually did attend. Matter of fact, I have required folks, several people to go to professional counseling. But, although I feel, I am a professional counselor, and feel that I can counsel as well as any professional counselor. I feel that the difference is that my first priority is being a minister and with other obligations, I felt that X. needed someone to deal directly with his case and would be available whenever he would be needed. Because this was a serious point in his life. I' somewhat hesitate to let a person just slip through the cracks. And so if, I see that I don't have the full knowledge of what they are dealing with, or full understanding then I will try to send them to a professional counselor. And he did go, matter of fact, he is still going at this time.

Interviewer:
Okay, is there another?

Pastor 2:
There is another case that I'm kind of dealing with but I really don't want to deal with, huh and it's a man in the church. His name is B., but it is a man in the church Brother B, he's gay. But he's trying to reform his life. My problem is, you know, I felt more comfortable with him going to a professional counselor also. Because I feel that although I do counsel him now at church, I counsel him on a limited level because I don't want to interfere with what is taking place with his

Appendix D 119

professional counselor. I have talked with the professional counselor and was able to get just a little information they don't want to share a whole lot and I understand that, but you know, huh, and I was somewhat disappointed with the professional counselor. I was the one that sent the person to them and they know that I am relating to the person and for me not to interfere with what the professional counselor was doing and is doing, it is some things, I don't want to say the wrong thing to B., that would mess up or interfere with what the professional counselor is saying to him. That is it. Other cases, I have had some people with extreme depression, some I've been able to counsel and work with, even one clergy person. That pastor, had depression, basically, I sent him to, I really had asked him to be committed for a while and he was at one of the hospitals in the city. I felt that was needed and so, since then I've talked with him but I don't counsel him.

Interviewer:
Right, Okay. Now, you've done quite a bit of counseling and still are doing counseling? Besides courses in seminary, what has been your training in counseling?

PASTOR 2:
Right. Experience.

Interviewer:
Experience?

PASTOR 2:
Uh, yes, experience. I think that the path of counseling, I have problems sometimes with what is called professional

counselors. Because a lot of times they use medicines and I think the only difference between a so-called professional counselor and myself who is professional, is the fact that they can write prescriptions and sometimes people who don't need prescription get prescriptions?

Interviewer:
Huh! Huh,

PASTOR 2:
And prescriptions keep a person sometimes in a condition and that person can never come out of that condition because they're dependent on that prescription. My thing is a person don't need a medicine to control them unless they really need a medicine to control them. And I think a lot of times we label folk and people come in and a lot of professional counselors take an easy way out and just put a person on medicine and that person really don't need a medicine they need counseling. They need someone to work some problems out with them. And I think that happened quite a bit. I've seen people who have taken medicine, and I'm not saying that there is not a point where it is needed. I do believe that a lot of people need medicine. I have several people here that are on depression medicine. Because they need it, they must have it. Huh, so, you know and I think that a lot of times I just want to make sure and when I see that or discern that in a person, I make sure that they go to another level.

Interviewer:
Are you familiar with pastoral counselor verses a psychiatrist? The psychiatrist is the only one who can prescribe medication.

Pastor 2:
Yes, right!

Interviewer:
Now are you familiar with the difference between a psychiatrist and a pastoral counselor?

Pastor 2:
Yes, right. Yes! I think the difference is a psychiatrist has gone through some medical points to understand emotions.

Interviewer:
Yes, you're right.

Pastor 2:
To understand emotions, to understand habits, to understand you know issues of the brain and what a person's going through. That's still good and that's I think that's the reason I asked this young man to commit himself to a hospital because I felt he needed that kind of help. When I see a person that, matter of fact, I know several folks now that I would talk to and I'm trying to talk them into going to a psychiatrist. Because there are some things that I can't do and I'm hoping that these are people I know need medicine. These are people I know that need to be treated. Some need to be huh, huh, I don't like this word so much and maybe you can give me a better word, but incarcerated in a health facility to give them help.

Interviewer:
Involuntary admissions to a psychiatric facility.

PASTOR 2:
Okay. Yeah, something like that. Pastoral counseling on a professional level, I think are pastors who have gone the extra mile to get an understanding of the issues, huh, sort of, what you're doing? Basically, but at the same time, still the best avenue to counseling to go along with the research and taking the time to go and to interview, is also experience. You got to be able to know people and discern emotions because as a pastor, huh, you got to be able to, if a person got a problem, you don't want that person walking around hurting themselves or hurting someone else. So basically, I try to deal with people with problems, marriage counseling, pre-marital counseling, adultery, some children issues. If a person has a problem that is going to be more extensive then I prefer they go to a pastoral counselor first. And maybe that person can, if they can't help then, they can recommend that they go to a psychiatrist.

Interviewer:
Now as far as your experience and your gifts as being a counselor, do you see a distinction in your gifts and graces and that of a pastoral counselor. And which type of person would you continue to work with and which would you refer to a pastoral counselor?

PASTOR 2:
I would try to work with everybody I can. A person that I discern that have a serious problem that needs more intentional help. I think they need to go to a person who is

designed just for pastoral counseling. Now, I'm a pastoral counselor but my designation right now is wide? And I'm saying a pastoral counselor as a person who's focused in taking care of the needs of this person. So, if I feel and I would do that in a moment? Because I care about the person and I don't want to mess with someone and give them wrong advice. So if I see that they need some more structure. Then that person, even if it's a marriage counselor, even if it is pre-marital, because you got some people set on getting married that if I can't talk to them then need to deal with a pastoral counselor that is geared to just dealing with what they are going through.

Interviewer:
Okay, now I want to be clear about this because there are pastors who counsel and then there are pastoral counselors but from what've I've understood you to say you are a pastoral counselor? Not a pastor who counsels?

Pastor 2:
Right, I agree with that, there are pastors who counsel and I am a pastoral counselor. And I feel that my success rate in counseling folk is probably greater than most folk that counsel.

Interviewer:
Huh, huh! Without the additional training?

Pastor 2:
Right.

Interviewer:

Did you take any additional pastoral counseling courses in seminary?

PASTOR 2:

I did that was one of my areas of ministry and I took some extended pastoral counseling. Because I was concerned about that, matter of fact, I worked in institutions in Atlanta just dealing with pastoral counseling. And I did some extra work, some continuing education dealing with that because I feel that we're living in a time where people actually need some help. But still I don't think I know everything and I'm not as detailed as I want to be so I still have to lean to other folk because I care about the people first.

Interviewer:

Now, in the professional pastoral counselor field, they feel that pastors should not provide pastoral counseling because it develops a dual relationship where a parishioner, meaning they not only see you as pastor but if you have this other relationship where you are their counselor, that there might cause some problems, they might worry that something they might share with you in the counseling room might come out in a sermon, or you know, might be shared somewhere else. What do you think about that?

PASTOR 2:

First of all, I agree with that that can happen. And a lot of times, it may not even be that the pastor has actually brought up anything that came out in counseling. But the pastor could just be delivering his sermon from God and a sermon that was prepared based on what God had given him or her and if you relate to that, that person will quickly say you talked about me in your sermon and that happens. I've experienced that will happen. That is a danger in that and you have to be able to combat that. Because I don't think that if you are going to be a pastor preaching, you can just say what you not going to preach because it might hit somebody. And a lot of times, you are not thinking about that it's going to hit somebody. But I think that is why I say, if anything that is deep or intentional, where a person needs some serious one on one, they need to be with a pastoral counselor and that's one of the reasons that I would do that in a minute; and I do send them to a pastoral counselor. Especially, somebody that's not relating.

Interviewer:
Now you said you counsel not only members of your church and you have a fairly large membership church in relationship to African-American churches, but you also counsel members of even larger churches, so how do you think you get those referrals?

Pastor 2:
I don't know, I being kind of wondering about that. Matter of fact, about once or twice a week I'm counseling some of X church members and Y church members. I do most of wedding counseling. Pre-marital counseling for some of those churches. Huh and people, they call me, I seek no one.

Interviewer:
Do you think that those people coming from those other churches, now I know about X church, I am familiar with their situation? Their pastor really doesn't do any counseling.

But some of these other churches do you think that people come to you because they don't want to bring those issues to their pastor? Or they took them to the pastor and the pastor said that he couldn't help them?

Pastor 2:
I think some are that they didn't want to bring the issues to the pastor. Some is that the pastor's fees are so high, huh; some is that the pastor gives them to another preacher, huh, some is you know they don't want it. I'm sure some of my members probably have some issues they would rather go to someone else than to come to me. You know I've counseled just last week a couple, premarital counseling, which I required eight sessions. But we counseled last week a couple from West Tennessee, who drove all the way here just to be counseled, I couldn't believe that. I didn't know the couple, but they had heard about some of the counseling sessions so.

Interviewer:
So in some of these other churches pastor charge their members for counseling?

Pastor 2:
Charge their members for counseling. If I charge someone, I'm going to send them to you. So, because I feel that, when a person has that need, they need to be with someone, if they are going to pay, they need someone directly toward that counseling need.

Interviewer:
Now as far as people coming to counseling do you see a difference between women and men? Do you think it is about the same?

Pastor 2:
More women come first.

Interviewer:
Do you have any reason why you think that's the case?

Pastor 2:
I think women for premarital counseling. I think women want to do the right thing. And, then I think that you have more women in church and so a church person is going to be more likely wanting to be in order. I think that has a lot to do with it.

Interviewer:
As far as when you make referrals. Who accepts and actually follow through on a referral. Man or women and why do you think that?

Pastor 2:
Both because what happens if the couple, if I refer a couple to a pastoral counselor or to a psychiatrist or to a hospital or something. I would follow up but I won't counsel them again because I really want them to get the more intentional help.

Interviewer:
Right, right.

Pastor 2:
They need that.

Interviewer:
You had mentioned one person that you referred to a counselor but you were a little frustrated with the counselor. Was that because you weren't getting any feedback?

Pastor 2:
It was that the person was talking to me on occasions with questions and I wanted, you know, I believe in the pastoral counselor or the psychiatrist, a relationship with their client, I don't have a problem with that. I do have a problem when I recommend someone to somebody and they know that I still have a relationship with that person and I'm trying to help them, I'm not trying to undermine them, I'm trying to help them so I don't want to give them bad advice and if a person comes back to me and say what do I do in this case and you (professional counselor) tell me I can't tell you nothing. You (professional counselor) just tell them to come to me. I don't have time for you. I will not recommend nobody else to go to that person.

Interviewer:
Okay, let me make sure that I understand if they come to you for advice or they come to you for something else?

Pastor 2:
Okay, the person I was counseling.

Interviewer:
Right.

Pastor 2:

I deemed that that person needed professional help. I sent them to a either a professional counseling service in this case it was a professional counseling service, but it was a professional pastoral counselor. But the person is still a member of my church and I'm trying to work with the professional pastoral counselor, I don't want to know what you talked about, I don't want to know what you're telling that person, I don't want to know your relationship with the person. I'm saying, I'm asking the professional counselor, what to do, so I do not undermine you and not to go against you but to help this person. And that professional counselor tells me, "I can't tell you nothing, you need just tell him to come to me." I said okay, you need to go to them but I wont recommend nobody else to that professional counselor. Because I felt the professional counselor disrespected me, in me trying to help them, and the person. They were more concerned about their fee to me than the person and I was upset about that and I'm still upset about that, but that person can't get another person from me. I think people are more than money. I think that you want to help a person. I was not trying to undermine the professional counselor. I was not trying to take anything away from them, but I have a responsibility to my members and so if my members say something. You know, well tell them to do this until they can get back me. Encourage them in this manner. I'm could have gave him advice. I didn't want to do that because they were going to a professional counselor. So my thing was don't give him advice because I don't know what the professional counselor had saw. The professional counselor might have given him some advice they did not like so they wanted me to give them something else. So I didn't want to give them something else without the professional counselor's knowledge. So that's all I was trying to do.

Interviewer:
The professional counselor didn't say, have them sign a release of information form then we can talk freely and work as a team.

Pastor 2:
I didn't really want to work as a team. I wanted the person to be with the professional counselor. I just know that I have a responsibility for my flock and when my flock asks me something. I'm trying to relate to them because I knew if I had not known that this person was with a professional counselor it would have been a different story. But since I knew that this person with a professional counselor, and I had sent them to the professional counselor, I'm just trying to be in order.

Interviewer:
Right.

Pastor 2:
I was not trying to be out of order. I don't want to take your client. I don't want to get involved, but I need to say other than you can't tell me nothing, just tell him to come to me, make an appointment and come to me.

Interviewer:
Tell me something, do you feel that because you are the shepherd of this congregation that people come to you for counseling because you are God's representative? And so they feel

that if anyone can help them, it would be the pastor of the church. Do you feel that is the reason people come to you for counseling. They see you in that light.

PASTOR 2:
Most definitely and I think a trust level has been built. Because I been here a good while.

Interviewer:
Do you feel like in their psychic, because black people traditionally keep their issues within the family? Do you feel that when they come to you as the pastor, they see you as an extension of the family, or do they see you just as the pastor and that's enough for them.

PASTOR 2:
I think they see me as the pastor and someone concerned about them.

Interviewer:
Huh, if you thought you were in need of any type of counseling would you go to a professional counselor or would you go to another clergy person.

PASTOR 2:
At this point, I would go to a professional counselor, but I'll tell you why?
I don't trust, huh, the clergy people that I know. If I had a trust level of clergy, then I would go to a clergy. Because I don't have that trust level, huh, I would go to a professional counselor.

Interviewer:
So, it really is more of a trust level than the training of the counselor related to the issue you are dealing with?

Pastor 2:
If, you know, it depends too. You know that would be a second point if it depends on the issue.

Interviewer:
If it was more that you felt emotional, psychological, stress related which one would you go to?

Pastor 2:
I'd go to a professional.

Interviewer:
If you thought it was more spiritual or just burnout?

Pastor 2:
If its burnout, I'm still going to a professional.

Interviewer:
Okay, when would you think you would go to a clergy, if there were one that you could trust?

Pastor 2:
If I had a relationship problem, I would go to a clergy. If I had something was stressing me in the church; I would go to a clergy. Ha.

Interviewer:
I just have a few other follow-up questions just to get your thoughts on. Do you feel that African-Americans think that

it's the pastor's responsibility to provide for their mental, emotional and spiritual needs?

Pastor 2:
Yes,

Interviewer:
Why?

Pastor 2:
The pastor has been in the African-American church; the pastor has been all of that. And we as African-Americans, until recently, haven't had access to professional counseling or a psychiatrist. That has just recently come about and so still; you don't have enough professional counselors that's out there for African-American so all of that is put on their pastor.

Interviewer:
Okay, when you said enough pastoral counselors or counselors out there. You talking about other African-American pastoral counselors?

Pastor 2:
Right. Are available to African Americans.

Interviewer:
Okay, do you think that it is the clergy's responsibility to meet their mental and emotional needs?

Pastor 2:
I think that to an extent. I think to an extent it is our responsibility.

Interviewer:

Do you think when African Americans come to the pastor for counseling they want concrete advice or do you think that they really want insight into why they do the things they do and are experiencing?

Pastor 2:

I think a lot of times, they want concrete advice, but then some do want insight into why is this? Another thing, you know I found out that a lot of people who come to pastor for counseling. I think that when they come to the pastor for counseling they can do it or not do. So they don't have to owe me because a lot of times they look at it as not official.

Interviewer:

That's good insight. Huh, do you think African Americans reject childhood experiences as being a problem that they might be dealing with in their adult life now. Do they just dismiss that as if they have an issue with trust, or if they have other issues that might stem from some childhood experience, do you think African-American's reject that whole notion or not?

Pastor 2:

I think that in some cases they do and some they don't. I think that's almost 50–50. I 'm seeing that a lot of people now are relating to what happen in childhood. Awhile back, people were fearful of relating their childhood to their actions now. But now more and more people will accept, you know, I'm this way you know, it goes back to experiences from my childhood.

Interviewer:
Why do you think that they were hesitate? Do you have any insight on that?

Pastor 2:
Because people did not want to for one, they didn't want to relive that childhood experience. Two, I think because they didn't want to convict some folks that probably could have been convicted, not through law but within their hearts and within themselves. So for those reasons they hesitated to talk about it.

Interviewer:
Okay, do you know of any African-American counselors that are in the community providing counseling that you would refer to?

Pastor 2:
Pastoral counselors?

Interviewer:
Yes, Professional?

Pastor 2:
Maybe two, three but they are not in Nashville.

Interviewer:
I'm talking about in our community.

Pastor 2:
No!

Interviewer:
Okay, there are none out there or none that you would refer to?

Pastor 2:
There are none out there.

Interviewer:
Okay. Have you ever experiences anyone refusing a referral?

Pastor 2:
Yes, on a few occasions.

Interviewer:
Do you think shame had anything to do with it?

Pastor 2:
Yes, it had a lot to do with some, probably cost, and some was very resentful and upset with me for referring them to the counselor.

Interviewer:
I guess that is about it Pastor 2 unless you have anything else to add, thank you.

Appendix E

INTERVIEW QUESTIONNAIRE FOR PASTORS PARTICIPATING IN THE STUDY

Please share two or three stories about individuals coming to you for pastoral counseling and whether you were able to help them or referred them to an appropriate trained counseling professional in the community. If they resisted the referral to a professional counselor what do you believe were the reasons for their resistance?

All parishioners' identities will be kept concealed. In order to achieve this objective you will be directed at the beginning of the interview process not to use real names or any identifying information, if necessary the circumstances in the stories may be changed to protect the identity of the parishioner. Persons in the congregation who sought counseling will not be identified personally in any reports or publications resulting from this project. Any identifying characteristics will also be modified.

The following are possible follow-up questions depending on the response to the above inquiry.

(1) Why do you think people who seek counseling from the pastor will not accept a referral to a pastoral counselor or other counseling professional?

FOLLOW-UP QUESTIONS:

  A. Do you think men or women are more receptive to counseling? Why?

  B. Do you think men or women are more receptive to referrals? Why?

  C. In what cases would you provide counseling and in what cases would you attempt to refer?

(2) Do African Americans view professional counseling as alien since families and churches deal with their inner personal concerns?

FOLLOW-UP QUESTIONS:

  A. Do you feel African Americans think it is the pastor's responsibility to provide for their mental, emotional, and spiritual needs? Why?

  B. Do you feel it is the pastor's responsibility to meet their mental and emotional needs? Why?

  C. Is it your experience that African Americans want concrete advice? Why?

  D. Is it your experience that African Americans often reject childhood interpretations of problems? Why?

- E. Do you think African American believe white counselors will not be understanding or culturally sensitive?
- F. If there were qualified African American pastoral counselors would parishioners seek help from them?

(3) *Why do you think some African American parishioners reject referrals to trained professional counselors?*

FOLLOW-UP QUESTIONS:

- A. To what degree does shame play a role in refusing a referral?
- B. What role does economic status play in coming to the pastor for help?
- C. To what degree do parishioners believe the pastor is God's representative and will know how to help them without going to a professional counselor?

(4) *Do you define pastoral counseling as the act of receiving personal advice from your pastor, any pastor or a member of the clergy inside or outside of the church? Why?*

FOLLOW-UP QUESTIONS:

- A. If your answer is yes what is the difference between pastoral counseling in the parish and pastoral counseling in a professional center?
- B. How do you define pastoral counseling?

(5) *What professional counseling resources are available in your community?*

A. If there are professional counseling resources have you or would you make referral there?

B. What relationship have you developed with these professionals?

Bibliography

Azlin, Cheryl R. "Attitudes of Fundamentalist Pastors toward the Causes and Treatment of Mental Illness." *Dissertation Abstracts International,* 1993, Vol. 53, p. 4942.

Bentz, W. K. and Edgerton, J. W. "Consensus on Attitudes Toward Mental Illness Between Leaders and the General Public in a Rural Community." *Archives of General Psychiatry,* 1970, Vol 22, p. 468.

Body-Franklin, Nancy. *Black Families in Therapy: Understanding The African American Experience.* (New York: The Guilford Press 2003) p. 23.

Cafferky, M. E. "Whole Health Education The Religious Workers Role." *Health Education,* 1982, Vol. 23, No 2, pp. 25–27.

Clebsch, William A., and Jaekle, Charles R. *Pastoral Care In Historical Perspective.* (Northvale, New Jersey: Rowman and Littlefield Publishers, Inc. 1983) pp. 13–14.

Curry, Jason Richard. *Exploring The Correspondence Between The Preferences Of African-American Congregants And The Tenets Of Prevalent Pastoral Theologians: A Metropolitan Study In Kentucky.* Dissertation (Vanderbilt University, May 2005) pp. 24–25.

Fairbank, Joel K. "Integration of Counseling Services Within the Church: Development of a Church Assistance Plan." *American Journal of Pastoral Counseling,* Vol. 3(2) 2000, pp. 43–47.

Greenspan, S.H. and Fuchs, A.D. "The Rabbi and The Psychiatrist Effective Counseling for Youth." *Journal of Religion and Health,* 1978, Vol 42, pp. 4370A-4371A.

Gurin, G., Veroff, J and Feld,S. *Americans View Their Mental Health A Nationwide Interview Survey.* (New York, NY Wiley, 1960).

Hembree, Daniel Troy. *Person, Community and Divinity in Yoruba Religious Thought and Culture: Foundations for Pastoral Theology*

With African American Men. Dissertation (Northwestern University 2003) p. 172.

Hohmann, A. A. and Larson, D. B. "Psychiatric Factors Predicting Use of Clergy." in E. L. Worthington, Jr. (Ed.), *Psychotherapy and Religious Values* (Grand Rapid, MI: Baker Book House, 1993), pp. 71–84.

Hunter, Rodney J. Dictionary Of Pastoral Care And Counseling. (Nashville, Abingdon Press, 1990) pp. 574–75.

Hyman, Bill, MS., Wylie, Wayne E., ED. D. "Implications For Improved Pastoral Health Counseling." (Texas A and M University College of Education, Department of Health and Physical Education 1987) pp. 162–68.

Lincoln, C. Eric and Mamiya, Lawrence H. *The Black Church in the African American Experience.* (Duke University Press 1990) p. 136.

McCann, R. .V. *The Churches and Mental Health.* (New York, NY Basic Books, 1962).

Meylink, Willa D., and Forsuch, Richard L., "Relationship between Clergy and Psychologists: The Empirical Data." *Journal of Psycholgy and Christianity*, 1988, Vol. 7, pp. 56–72.

Moessner, Jeanne Stevenson. *The Handbook of Womencare: Through the Eyes of Women Insights For Pastoral Care.* (Minneapolis: Fortress Press 1996) pp. 241–42.

Pruyser, P. W. *The Minister as Diagnostician.* (Philadelphia, PA Westminster Press, 1976), p. 47.

Richardson, Bernard Lester. "The Attitudes of Black Clergy and Parishioners towards Mental Illness and Mental Health Professionals." *Dissertation Abstracts International,* 1982, Vol. 43, p. 1192.

Ruppert, P. P., and Rogers, M. L. "Needs Assessment in the Development of A Clergy Consultation Service A Key Informant Approach." *Journal of Psychology and Theology,* 1985, Vol. 13, No 1, pp. 50–60.

Taylor, Steven J., and Bogdan, Robert. *Introduction To Qualitative Research Methods.*(New York, John Wiley and Sons, Inc., 1998) pp. 7–10.

The Holy Bible. New Revise Standard Version. Luke 4:18–19, Mathew 11:28–30 and John 3:5–6 (Nashville: Holman Bible Publishers, 1989).

Weaver, A. J. "Mental Health Issues Among Clergy and Other Religious Professionals: A Review of Research." *Journal of Pastoral Care,* 2002, Vol. 56 No.4, pp. 401–3.

Weaver, A. J., Koenig, H. G., and Larson, D. B. "Marital and Family Therapist and the Clergy: A Need for Clinical Collaboration, Training and Research." *Journal of Marital and Family Therapy,* 1997, Vol.23, No.1, pp.13–25.

Weaver, A. J., Revilla, L. A., and Koenig, H. G. *Counseling Families Across the Stages of Life: A Handbook for Pastors and Other Helping Professionals.* (Nashville,TN: Abingdon Press, 2002) p. 19.

West, Donnie W. Ph.D. "African-American Clergy's Perception of the Leading Health Problems in Their Communities and Their Role in Supporting Parishioner' Health." *The Journal of Pastoral Care and Counseling,* 2006 Vol. 60 p.16.

Wicks, Robert J., Parsons, Richard D., and Capps, Donald E. *Clinical Handbook of Pastoral Counseling.* (New York, Paulist Press, 1985) p. 309.

Wimberly, Edward P. *Pastoral Care in the Black Church.* (Nashville, TN Abingdon Press, 1979), p. 37.

Wimberly, Edward P. *Prayer in Pastoral Counseling Suffering, Healing and Discernment.* (Louisville: Westminster/John Knox Press 1990) pp. 13–14.

Wimberly, Edward P. *Using Scripture in Pastoral Counseling.* (Nashville, Abingdon Press: 1994) pp. 21–25.

Wylie, W. E. "Health Counseling Competencies Needed By the Minister." *Journal of Religion and Health,* 1984, Vol. 23, No 3, pp. 237–48.

www.ingramcontent.com/pod-product-compliance
Lightning Source LLC
Chambersburg PA
CBHW072141160426
43197CB00012B/2192